"Know-It-Alls"
How to Shut Them Up *Respectfully*!

Joe Ike

Copyright © 2012 Joe Ike. All Rights Reserved.

This publication may not be reproduced, transmitted, stored, copied or screen printed in part or in whole, in any form or by any means manual, electronic, mechanical or otherwise, without the express and prior written consent from the publisher and author. Brief quotations may be included in a review or as citations. If in PDF form, it may be stored as downloaded on your computer. One copy of this book may be printed for your own personal reading or use.

Disclaimer

The information and suggestions contained in this book are based on the author's opinion, experience, knowledge, education and background. The publishers and author are not liable for the use or misuse of the information and suggestions herein proffered.

Dedication

This book is dedicated to my wife for her doting love and support and to my friends for believing.

Table of Contents

Dedication ...3
Table of Contents ...4
Introduction ...9
  Chapter 1: What do people all over the world talk about? ...13
  Chapter 2: Do you know someone who is a Know-It-All? ...23
    Conversation Samples ...23
    What is the definition of a Know-It-All? ...26
    Who is a Know-It-All? ...29
    Narcissism and Aspergers Syndrome ...31
    Is technology fueling the Know-It-All behavior? ...33
Chapter 3: How Know-It-All's Acquire and Dispense Knowledge ...37
    The anatomy of a Know-It-All's knowledge ...38
    The primary conversation characteristics of a Know-It-All ...39
    The Know-It-All's verbal and non-verbal communication medium of disseminating knowledge ...43
    The Know-It-All's electronic and online communication medium of disseminating knowledge ...47
    The conversational settings where Know-It-Alls disseminate knowledge ...55
    The audience of a Know-It-All ...60
    The Know-It-All's knowledge cycle ...61
Chapter 4: Types of Know-It-All ...62

The Know-It-All Backseat Driver ...62
The Know-It-All Armchair Quarterback ...64
The Know-It-All Co-worker ...65
The Know-It-All Employee ...66
The Know-It-All Boss ...67
The Know-It-All Teacher 69
The Know-It-All Student ...71
The Know-It-All Boyfriend ...72
The Know-It-All Girlfriend ...75
The Know-It-All Husband ...76
The Know-It-All Wife ...78
The Know-It-All Friend ...80
The Know-It-All Neighbor 83
The Know-It-All Stranger ...85
The Know-It-All Mother ...87
The Know-It-All Father ...89
The Know-It-All Child ...91
The Know-It-All Brother or Sister ...93
The Know-It-All Forum or Chat Room Geek ...94
The Know-It-All Social Networker ...96

Chapter 5: The Know-It-Alls' Domain or Body of Knowledge ...102
Grammar ...102
Manners ...103
Opinion ...104
Weight ...105
Fashion ...105
Current Affairs or News ...106
Science and Technology ...107
Trivia ...108
Personal Dirt ...108
Politics ...109
Diet ...109
Race ...110
Gender ...111
Sports ...112

Sexuality ...112
Internet ...113
Business/Finance/Money ...114
Health ...115
Computer ...116
Hobby 117

Chapter 6: Manifestations of the Know-It-All Behavior ...119
Obsessed with corrections ...121
Domineering ...123
Faultfinding ...125
Condescending ...126
Projecting flaws and self criticism onto others ...128
Manipulative and controlling ...129
Hypercritical ...132
Pompous 133
Exaggerating ...135
An Unsolicited spokesperson ...136
Prone to lies ...138
Overly assertive ...140
Self-centered ...141
Obnoxious ...143
Obsessed with perfection in words, thoughts and deeds ...144
Bully ...147

Chapter 7: How Know-It-Alls Make Us Feel ...151
Annoyed ...152
Frustrated ...153
Denigrated ...153
Defensive ...154
Ignored ...155
Tired ...156
Intimidated ...157
Dumb ...159
Manipulated ...160
Controlled ...161

Shoved off the limelight ...163
Nit-picked out of our wits ...164
Bullied ...165
Flustered ...166
Patronized ...167
Insulted ...168
Embarrassed ...171
Hindered by ineffective communication ...172
Humiliated ...173

Chapter 8: Why Do Know-It-Alls Behave Like They Do? ...176

Are you a Know-It-All? ...176
Some reasons why Know-It-Alls behave like they do ...178
    Insensitive ...178
    Insecure ...179
    Narcissistic ...181
    Poor communication skill ...183
    Low self esteem ...184
    Obsessed with perfection ...185
    Inordinate desire to manipulate and control others ...186
How to stop the Know-It-All behavior ...187
    Listen attentively ...188
    Communicate openly ...189
    Do not dominate conversations ...191
    Recognize the signs and control your Know-It-All impulses ...192
    Accept responsibility ...193
    Stop obsessing over trivial details ...194
    Don't use your knowledge to humiliate and intimidate ...196
    Avoid brutal honesty ...197
    Discard negative and destructive criticism ...199
    Avoid or be cognizant of controversial subjects ...200

Chapter 9: "Know-It-Alls" – How to shut them up respectfully! ...203
   Be verbally firm and direct ...205
   Identify the warning signs and take action ...208
   Request for the source of information ...210
   Don't walk into the argument trap ...212
   Use humor effectively ...214
   Remind them that they are human ...216
   Propose alternative ideas ...218
   Introduce subjects outside their domain of knowledge ...220
   Reject negative criticism ...221
   Use questions and comments effectively ...223
   Be assertive and convincing ...225
   Listen and do not interrupt ...227
   Change the subject ...229
   Strongly convey your disapproval ...231
   Be patient and understanding ...232
   Journalize the humiliating conversations ...234
   Refuse to be rudely interrupted ...235
   Do not respond to a bully ...237
   Stay away from controversial subjects ...239
   Walk away ...240
Notes ...241

Introduction

Who should read this book? Everyone should read this book, including you and me. Why? Because we have all met, work with, possibly live with, and will yet meet a Know-It-All in the course of our life time. In fact, if you lean over and asked the person seated or standing next to you at this moment, if he or she has ever met a Know-It-All, the probability is that the answer will be a rotund YES! Furthermore, most people know and remember vividly the feeling of discomfort and tense trepidation that lasts the duration of an encounter with a Know-It-All.

One of the most complained about and denigrating social issue that impacts human relationships and friendships is the Know-It-All behavior in all its manifestations. Scouring through literally millions of Know-It-All related complaints from people of all walks of life, gender and culture helps one to comprehend the magnitude of this exasperatingly aggravating social problem. Most of these complaints, of course, are rarely mentioned during the office visits to psychologists and psychiatrists, but are openly confessed and tucked away in quasi-anonymous public forum postings, blogs, chat archives and social networking profile pages.

An interesting take on this issue is that, while people often visit psychiatrists and psychologists to consult about their aggression in any of its various manifestations, fewer people if any visit these professionals to consult about their Know-It-All behavior even when it is wrecking havoc in their personal life at home, school, workplace or social settings. There is a preponderance of evidence that indicates clearly, that a lot of Know-It-Alls are aware of their behavior and its impact on their victims.

This book is uniquely a first on many fronts, for example, chapter 1 of this book draws the reader into the book by numerically and textually illustrating the enormousness, ubiquity and global nature of the Know-It-All behavior. But the book does more than that, it defines the term Know-It-All, identifies who is a Know-It-All, enumerates in an anecdotic manner the different ways they manifest the Know-It-All behavior, recounts how the Know-It-All behavior makes us feel, details psychologist's recommendations for curtailing and stopping the Know-It-All behavior, and finally empowers victims with 20 practical ways to peacefully and respectfully shut up a Know-It-All.

Most likely you have interacted with a Know-It-All today or in the recent past. Are men more likely than women to be Know-It-Alls? What is the most complained about manifestation of all the Know-It-All behaviors? Are people more annoyed with Know-It-Alls who constantly interrupt others to opine their "wisdom" or are people more upset with Know-It-Alls who are incessantly correcting other people like a machine gun stuck in a permanent firing mode? How do people generally feel in the presence of a Know-It-All? Do they feel that the Know-It-All is trying to control them or intimidate them? Of all the people we associate with on a daily basis who is most likely to be an agonizing Know-It-All? Who is more likely to be a Know-It-All between your best friend and your father? These questions and lots more are numerically and textually answered in the book.

This well researched book, with almost 300 references, is written in a way that takes cognizant of the fact that most readers today are web or internet savvy. Furthermore, today than any other time in the internet era, most people tend to look up "stuff" they read or talk about. This book is not an academic or psychology textbook and so the language and flow is adapted for relaxed, entertaining and sometimes very humorous reading. The humor infused within the various anecdotes and hyperboles gyrates around everyday life at home, at work, on the street and on the internet - particularly socializing on the internet. As entertaining as the anecdotes and hyperboles are, they are used to drive home the practical value of the points being made. When psychosocial issues are elucidated, psychological authorities are cited to buttress the facts presented.

As was alluded to earlier, there are literally millions of people who are anguished on a daily basis by the Know-It-All in their lives. These people have reached out to their various online forums for counsel or guidance or tip to help them survive the daily or frequent onslaught. Later in this book we will talk about these emotionally unsettling situations. Although there are books that have mentioned or discussed in passing the problem of having Know-It-Alls in our lives, none of those books are dedicated to this very serious problematic behavior or attitude that is making the lives of many people miserable.

This book moreover elaborates how technological advancements including cell phones, smart phones, the internet, chat rooms, text messages, instant messages, and public forums have indirectly exacerbated the

Know-It-All behavior by providing readily available information that arm Know-It-Alls and create a medium to dispense knowledge as a weapon of emotional obliteration. In other words, not only is information a click away, but Know-It-Alls have the added incentive of perceived anonymity and the wherewithal to impersonally or remotely deploy their "knowledge" laden missiles at a loved one, intimate friend or unsuspecting acquaintance.

Hundreds of authoritative psychological, psychiatric, advice, counsel, self-help and How-to books and journals had been scoured to sift out and hone information related to this Know-It-All behavior. Thousands of electronic data sources [websites, blogs, forum archives, chat archives and personal profiles] were rummaged to find out how people feel and have been impacted by this behavior specifically. The single goal has been to help us understand the behavior and take appropriate action to protect our sanity.

This book was not written to offer psychological or psychiatric advice, it is written from the point of view of someone who has experienced first hand the disastrous effects of a Know-It-All and simply describes what Know-It-Alls do to hurt us, make us feel unhappy, marginalize and denigrate us. It does not matter if this is done face to face or via email or chat rooms or forum posts or instant messaging or text messaging. The book then enumerates how we feel in those situations and most importantly provides practical ways to deal with the Know-It-All and bring back cheer to our lives. Of course we can help the Know-It-All search for psychiatric and psychological counselors, in the Yellow Pages if they prefer, since we may not want to admit to our favorite search engine that "we" are looking for eh..., well, a shrink!

Chapter 1: What do people all over the world talk about?

How would you answer the above question? For example, globally, do people talk more about politics or the subject of death in their conversations? What is the one topic or issue that globally dominates every conversation or personal thought? Undoubtedly, people talk about current newsworthy issues and people, but those generally tend to have a limited live span or scope, and current issues are constantly changing. For example, in every country and locality there are politicians, businesspeople, celebrities, etc. who are newsmakers. Additionally, local events like recent flooding, current politics, the latest crime, the current state of the economy and so on dominate the news, but the newsworthiness of these people, events and issues is continually changing.

Nonetheless, there are inherent important issues that people incessantly talk about in their households, workplace, public places, friendships, relationships and so forth. This is true in all cultures and nations at any point in time, even when the issues may not be part of the mainstream news. Naturally, some of these are controversial issues. [1] They include but are not limited to the economy, crime, love, school, money, politics, health, disease, religion, marriage, technology, date rape, child labor, gender, racial prejudice, religious prejudice (and other prejudices), abortion, animal cruelty, homosexuality, gun control, death penalty and so on. No doubt, you have talked about one or more of these issues recently or in the immediate past. While it is true that some issues may dominate our conversation and the news media in our country or locality, the fact is that such issues may not even make the front page in other countries and cultures.

Moreover, when people converse, are they talking "more" about money or health, gun control or the death penalty, abortion or homosexuality? How do we know if our own localized controversial issues are truly global in nature? Which issues are the most talked about all over the world? What is there rank of importance? The answers to these questions and especially there magnitude when ranked will help us to put the magnitude of Know-It-All behaviors in there apposite perspectives. In other words, how universally important or common are the Know-It-All behaviors? Are people talking or concerned about Know-It-Alls and the Know-It-All behaviors? Additionally, it will help answer questions like: Are men more likely than women to be Know-It-Alls? Between your best friend and your father who is more likely to be an agonizing Know-It-All?

How do we go about answering questions of this nature and universal magnitude? Obviously we cannot interview the earth's seven billion (or about) inhabitants. Paper surveys, web based surveys, email surveys, telephone surveys, one-on-one or face-to-face surveys with there various data collection methods are indispensible tools when the target population is relatively small. However, for our purposes a sample survey [2] will suffice, in other words, we can survey a representative portion of the world's population and then make educated inferences. Who comprises our target population? This is basically anybody who can converse or talk.

Is it not true that we write, email, journalize, text message, post message and publish subject matters and issues that preoccupy our daily thinking and dominate our daily conversation? Therefore, we can say that our target or survey population comprises the list of everybody who ever wrote about any subject under consideration, and today, a sizeable portion of that writing exists electronically on different computer based storages around the world. With the help of internet based search engines we can access these millions of writings and parse out information that helps us to find out what people are really talking about in the confines of their personal space, with friends, family, co-workers and so on. A sample as provided by the search engine results has advantages [3] over trying to survey the whole world and these advantages include the fact that it is more economical, a lot faster and very practical. Given the ubiquity of the English language, and the fact that even where it is not the official language [4] it is one of the languages spoken in some countries, we can assume that the English language web pages, returned in the search result set, are representative enough for our purposes.

The first step in the methodology used, entailed identifying a broad list of controversial issues. Next, each controversial issue was contextually searched and the number of results recorded. The number of results was then ranked and used to make educated inferences. For simplicity, only one search engine was used.

Are there precedents for this methodology and the type of inference made with the search engine results?

Yes there are, even though the levels of sophistication vary. The methodology used here is similar in principle to that used in the research [5, 6] communities where the number of papers published by a researcher and the number of citations of each of those published papers are used to rank or index the efficacy of the researcher. Furthermore, search engines, like Google's search engine, rank [7] pages based on how many other pages are linked to the page, among other factors. The more links there are on the internet that link to any one page, the higher the rank of that one page, in other words, the more other pages on the internet talk about a specific page, then the higher will be the ranking of that specific page.

To illustrate the foregoing, supposing you were having lunch with a close friend and the word "crime" or "love" or "spark plug" or "Know-It-All" occurred very frequently in her speech for that short duration, often we assume or conclude that this must be her current preoccupation. Now, if she chatted online, instant messaged, emailed, posted questions in an online forum, web logged or blogged, posted comments on her web page, journalized and so forth, the chances are those same words will be included in the content of the message. Deductively then, we can infer, albeit not perfectly, that the more pages there are on the internet on any subject the more important it is in the mind, thinking, preoccupation and conversations of people in general regardless of the culture or nation or locality. Hence, we can surmise that the total number of those pages, as represented in a web search result, is a good indicator of the level of importance in the mind, thinking, preoccupation and conversations of people.

Before we look at a few comparative result sets it is important to remember that the numbers should not be taken literally, since there may be overlaps, meaning that, infrequently some pages may be copies of each other but located on different computers. Furthermore, occasionally a page's context may not harmonize with the usage context we seek and some pages may contain postings from two or more people, although it is counted as one page. There are no statistical margins of error since these are simply rough order of magnitude estimates.

At the beginning of this chapter the following questions were raised: Do people talk more about politics or the subject of death in their conversations? What is the one topic or issue that globally dominates every conversation or personal thought? Are people talking more about money or health, gun control or the death penalty, abortion or homosexuality? Table 1 below answers these questions. Not only are there more pages and thought dedicated to the subject of death than politics, but the one issue that dominates every conversation, thought and writing is health. Some of the numbers, however, were expected. For example, while health and love preoccupy us more than money, it is interesting to note that more web pages, writing and thought were dedicated to money than religion or marriage or hunger or all three combined.

Did you notice in Table 1 also, that the expression or phrase Know-It-All, irrespective of the different ways people phrase it, ranked significantly higher than a lot of social issues that garner media attention? This is not a happenstance or coincidence. In fact, if you spent time and read through some of the millions of pages associated with that keyword, you will realize immediately that it is a pervading social issue deeply woven into the fabrics of marriages, relationships, friendships, and the workplace. Later in this book we will define the term Know-It-All, identify who is a Know-It-All, enumerate the different ways Know-It-Alls manifest the Know-It-All behavior, recount how the Know-It-All behavior makes us feel, detail some ways Know-It-Alls can curtail the behavior, and finally how to peacefully and respectfully shut up a Know-It-All or make them keep silent and leave us in peace.

One interesting take on this social issue of the Know-It-All behavior is that, while people often visit psychiatrists and psychologists to consult about their aggressive behavior in any of its various manifestations, fewer people if any visit these professionals to consult about their Know-It-All behavior even when it is wrecking havoc in their personal life; especially in the way they relate with others. Numerous postings on the issue indicate clearly that a lot of Know-It-Alls are aware of their behavior and its impact on their victims.

Table 1 - Table of Keywords of Some Controversial Social Issues

#	Keywords Searched	Result	#	Keywords Searched	Result
1	Health	2.52 billion	16	Hunger	32.5 million
2	Love	2.22 billion	17	"Sexual Abuse"	31.2 million
3	School	989 million	18	Aggression	23.6 million
4	Money	948 million	19	Abortion	19.2 million
5	Technology	855 million	20	Homosexuality	12.1 million

6	Jobs	850 million	21	"Death Penalty"	8.00 million
7	Sex	787 million	22	"Sexual Assault"	6.84 million
8	Food	744 million	23	"Child Labor"	2.48 million
9	Death	400 million	24	"Gun Control"	2.23 million
10	Politics	283 million	25	"Animal Cruelty"	2.05 million
11	Crime	276 million	26	"Date Rape"	1.10 million
12	Disease	228 million	27	"Racial Prejudice"	0.74 million
13	Economy	218 million	28	"Sexual Aggression"	0.39 million
14	Religion	213 million	29	"Religious Prejudice"	0.32 million
15	Marriage	129 million	30	"Gender Prejudice"	0.08 million
"Know-It-All" OR KnowItAll OR "Know All" OR KnowAll OR "Know It All"			125 million		

Source: Google.com search results - 01/07/2011

Let us spend a few moments and contrast this social issue, the Know-It-All behavior, with some mental health issues. Although statistically [8] speaking, only a few percent of people suffer from Schizophrenia in comparison to other forms of mental disorder, from Table 2 it can be seen that the amount of pages, thoughts, writings and comments dedicated to Schizophrenia is disproportionate. This is probably because of the disorder's debilitating impact. Nevertheless, the enormity of the Know-It-All behavior, simply from a numbers point of view, is evident when this social issue is compared with the mental disorder Schizophrenia.

Table 2 - Table of Keywords of Some Major DSM-IV Categories of Mental Disorders

#	Keywords Searched	Result	#	Keywords Searched	Result
1	Schizophrenia	17.5 million	7	"Borderline Personality Disorder"	1.06 million
2	"Bulimia Nervosa"	4.83 million	8	"Major Depressive Disorder"	1.04 million
3	"Bipolar Disorder"	4.56 million	9	"Common Anxiety Disorder"	0.50 million
4	"Anorexia Nervosa"	1.60 million	10	"Antisocial Personality Disorder"	0.34 million
5	"Panic disorder"	1.60 million	11	"Narcissistic Personality Disorder"	0.33 million
6	"Obsessive Compulsive Disorder"	1.58 million	12	"Histrionic Personality Disorder"	0.08 million

"Know-It-All" OR KnowItAll OR "Know All" OR KnowAll OR "Know It All"	125 million

Source: Google.com search results - 01/07/2011

Most likely you have interacted with a Know-It-All today or in the recent past. What is the most complained about manifestation of all the Know-It-All behaviors? Are people more annoyed with Know-It-Alls who constantly interrupt others to opine their "wisdom" or are people more upset with Know-It-Alls who are incessantly correcting other people like a machine gun stuck in a permanent firing mode? In chapter 6 the various manifestations of the Know-It-All behavior will be elucidated and the aforementioned questions will be answered.

How are people most likely to feel in the presence of a Know-It-All; controlled or intimidated? Are people more likely to complain about the humiliation they suffer in the presence of the Know-It-All or the fact that they cannot communicate effectively with the Know-It-All? In chapter 7 we will examine in detail the specific effects of the Know-It-All behavior on us and answer these fascinating questions raised here.

Finally, let us look at some of the most pertinent questions as it concerns Know-It-Alls. Of all the people we associate with on a daily basis who is most likely to be an agonizing Know-It-All? Who is more likely to be a Know-It-All between your best friend and your father, between you and your boyfriend or girlfriend, between you and your husband or wife, between a teacher and a student, between a mother and a father, between you and your brother or sister, between a friend and a stranger, between your boss and your husband or wife, between your boss and your co-worker? In chapter 4 we will answer these questions, enumerate the types of Know-It-Alls and expose some of their peculiar and sometimes downright raunchy behaviors. Furthermore, in chapter 4 we will answer the rather complex question: Are men more likely than women to be Know-It-Alls?

Now that we have looked at the prevalence of the Know-It-All behavior it is time to answer other ardent questions such as "What does the phrase Know-It-All mean?" "Who is a Know-It-All?" Really, who are they?

Chapter 2: Do you know someone who is a Know-It-All?

"Oh... I do!" is the overwhelming response heard whenever the above captioned question is asked, followed by narratives of irritation, annoyance, feelings of emotional and physical drain,, emotional hurt, and so forth. You most likely know one or several Know-It-Alls. The above stated reactions or effects of the Know-It-All behavior help us differentiate between normal forerunners or harbingers of knowledge and conceited Know-It-Alls. Before defining what constitutes the Know-It-All behavior or behaviors and who is a Know-It-All let us look at some everyday conversations.

Conversation Samples

Here are a few conversation samples that highlight the Know-It-All behavior.

> On a mild breezy autumn afternoon Tom and Mary were weeding their flower bed when an elderly couple alighted from a car parked a couple of houses over and walked to the front of Tom and Mary's house.

"Hi! Whereabouts is Rocking Hill Avenue?" The elderly lady asked.

"Rocking Hill Avenue?" Mary asked as she straightened up.

"Yes, please." The elderly lady answered.

"It's about two blocks from that stop sign," Mary pointed to the nearest stop sign in the direction the couple was facing. "There are gas stations at the Rocking Hill intersection …"

"No Mary, you're wrong. It's a little more than two blocks," interjected Tom abruptly cutting Mary off. "When you get to this stop sign," Tom continued, pointing and, walking towards the couple, "cross the intersection and continue straight down on this street. Walk on the right side of the street since it has more shade and watch out for a Rottweiler in the middle of the first block, the lavender colored house to be precise, 'cause they let that dog run lose at times. The home association has cited them many times and I tell you, they could care less if that dog bit someone. So far it hasn't and I bet it would one day. They never pay their dues regularly either. At the intersection of the first and second block, excuse the mess there, the homeowner at the corner house just moved into our area and …"

Superficially, it would seem as if Tom had provided useful details to the elderly couple. He provided the superfluous details and knowledge at what cost? It was provided at the cost of cutting off his wife in mid sentence, embarrassing her and dismissing her input in one fell swoop. Why? So he could sound off his well grounded knowledge of his neighborhood trivia that meant nothing to the strangers but means the world to him.

John and Emily his girlfriend hang out from time to time with Tony and Angela who are also dating. They do what most young people do when they hang out; converse.

"John how was your day at work today with crazy Bill?" Tony asked.

"Oh my boss… It was a quiet and peaceful day. He was not at work today."

"Yes he was!" Emily quipped in, staring fixedly at John with eyebrows raised.

"No he was not at work today," John replied with a puzzled look on his face, slightly embarrassed at the affront.

"That's his boss Emily, shouldn't he know if his boss came to work," Angela asked with a smile.

"I know for sure he came to work today. Ask me how I know."

The three stared at Emily.

Emily ransacked her purse and pulled out her cell phone. "When I called your work phone four times and your phone kept going to voicemail you sent me this text message – 'I am on the phone with crazy Bill' – so don't play selective amnesia with me… Ok!"

"Honey, Bill is on vacation. He called me from a beach tavern in Bora Bora. You know he is a micromanager and he kept me for over an hour on that call."

"Whatever. If he called you, it don't matter where he is, he was at work. That is why it is called Paid Time Off. Besides, I know you, when Bill does not come to work, you normally leave at midday. Today you did not, did you?"

John scratched his head, Tony stared off somewhere above Emily's head and Angela checked her timepiece and cleared her throat.

Is it not frustrating when your sincere and truthful comments or observations are discarded summarily and justified by defective reasoning? It can also be irritating when it seems your loved one knows more about an event that happened to you when and where they were not around. It is even worse when your loved one uses knowledge of your habits and quirks gathered over time against you, with the intent to win an argument at all cost.

What is the definition of a Know-It-All?

Before defining what the phrase Know-It-All means, it is best to start with what it does not mean since the phrase can also be used sometimes with a positive connotation when referring to someone endowed with knowledge in various subject matters or areas. Hence, we are not talking about someone with a strong opinion about things, or someone passionate about a subject matter and who expresses there conviction clearly, firmly and respectfully. In fact, there are countless knowledge fountains tucked away in Know-It-All books, Know-It-All quizzes and even Know-It-All websites that cater to information for specialized knowledge areas.

Consequently, a Know-It-All is not someone who is knowledgeable or a subject matter expert [1].

Here is a humorous but precise definition of a Know-It-All from John Wade's article titled "The know-it-all Syndrome":

"According to the psychologists we interviewed, most people who suffer from the know-it-all syndrome—whether a Webster who actually knows what [he or] she's talking about or merely a Clavin who pretends to know—have one personality trait in common: narcissism. Hiding behind the need to let the world know exactly how smart, how funny, how interesting or how great they are, is the need to convince themselves of their own value. All know-it-alls suffer from a lack of self-esteem, and what they seek, through their tireless attempts to impress, is usually approval and validation. As a result, the know-it-all usually chooses to surround herself with friends and mates who are appreciative—and may be even admiring—of [his or] her "knowledge.""" [2]

The connotative words "Webster", as in the dictionary name, and "Clavin", referring to the character Cliff Clavin in the television series sitcom called Cheers have been used to refer and distinguish between those who are truly endowed with mental acumen; and those who pretend to be knowledgeable. The point though is that the two groups are capable of becoming pejorative Know-It-Alls at the drop of a hat.

Dictionary.com defines a Know-It-All as "a person who acts as though he or she knows everything and who dismisses the opinions, comments, or suggestions of others." [3] This definition is very telling. Note that Know-It-Alls "act", meaning they are putting up a show or display of knowing, perhaps pretending to be an expert in what they are talking about. In reality however, perhaps by the gaffs they commit while talking or the lack of harmony in the details, it is evident that they are pretending to be knowledgeable and the knowledge being dispensed is pejorative. [4] The definition also encompasses one of the most frequently heard complaints, that is, dismissing the opinion, comments, contributions, views, counsel and suggestions of others as, of course, being of no consequence. This is true even when others are more educated than the Know-It-All and perhaps more intelligent than the Know-It-All. [5] Consequently, the level of intelligence or education of the Know-It-All in relation to his audience is not the primary factor for exhibiting the Know-It-All behavior. In fact, preteen [6] kids have been known to exhibit the Know-It-All behavior, as well as the extremely intelligent or brainiacs. [7]

The intent of the knowledge being dispensed by the Know-It-All most often is pejorative, in other words, as Dictionary.com defines it, "having a disparaging, derogatory, or belittling effect or force." [8] Later in this book, we will see other effects of the Know-It-All behavior, however it is pertinent to point out that the behavior is not restricted to a specific gender. Males and females exhibit the Know-It-All behavior, and so do the upper social cadre or high socio-economic status, the so-called elite class. [9]

There are other interesting words that have been used informally to describe persons who demonstrate the Know-It-All behavior. These include pedantic [10], hypercritical, and Know-All. These descriptive words lay bare other manifestations of the Know-It-All behavior as perceived by the observers. Now imagine for a moment, living with or working with or having a friend who is pedantic, obsessed with minutiae and who is also hypercritical. For some folks, that is their daily bread and butter! Other synonyms used to informally describe persons who display the Know-It-All behavior include: "polymath, smarty pants, smart aleck, wise guy, clever dick, wisenheimer, smarty, and wisecracker." [4] You probably know a lot of other words and expressions.

Perhaps one of the most annoying manifestations of the Know-It-All behavior is that of accumulating useless, negative, trivial, intimate and downright embarrassing private information of friends or family or workmates over time and then consistently drawing down on that knowledge to denigrate, humiliate and ultimately control the outcome of everyday conversation or steer the direction of the conversation towards selfish gains. This is one of the most annoying Know-It-All behaviors because it's something that we could experience at close quarters everyday, until it becomes a personal affront. [11] Furthermore, it is one of the worst manifestations of the Know-It-All behavior because the Know-It-All will air your private and dirty laundry in public and on the internet if that is the only way to show off their grisly knowledge, win an argument and defend their point of view and in doing so humiliate you. [12]

Who is a Know-It-All?

We can surmise the answer to this question from the various definitions above. There is no doubt that Know-It-Alls have spent some time acquiring knowledge, both useful and useless. Useless, especially if the knowledge serves no other purpose than to denigrate or disparage others. Since Know-It-Alls have the tendency to impress, they will likely be on the prowl for information both positive and negative and accumulate this, with the intent to offload the knowledge at an opportune or inopportune moment. Having invested so much time and effort acquiring such knowledge they become fanatical or obsessive about every subject, issue or situation they have researched or heard or accumulated and as such, quickly dismiss opposing views or even appropriate corrections to their strongly entrenched viewpoint. This dismissal, tacitly or expressed, is usually the first source of conflict and alienation between Know-It-Alls and their audience.

Even when no conflict arises, their listeners will most likely move into a passive listening mode, mentally ceding the conversation and center stage, as it were, to them. It is in circumstances such as this that Know-It-Alls' monopolized conversations turn into one-way monologues [7] and listeners "suffer" through a session of lecturing, perhaps laced with condescending expletives cleverly camouflaged as part of the knowledge dissemination session.

To illustrate the perspective of the Know-It-All's audience or listener, imagine for a moment your favorite automatic beverage dispenser at home or at work. Several times a day you traipse over to the dispenser, dispense a cup and return to your desk or favorite sofa to savor the beverage. One day, after dispensing a cup, the dispenser will not shut off automatically, and so you quickly gulp down the beverage and try to catch some of the beverage being wasted while you try to figure out how to turn of the dispenser manually. By the time you figure out and turn off the dispenser manually, the counter top and carpet is a gooey and slushy mess. Most likely, the cup you gulped down in a rush and the cup you saved from waste way may not be as savory as the previous cups dispensed to you in the past. The point is, while a Know-It-All may have dispensed very much needed and beneficial knowledge in the past, the moment knowledge dispensing sessions turn into one-way condescending monologues the listeners will get their full and the rest of the knowledge gets wasted or provokes averse feelings which we will elaborate on much later in this book.

It can be succinctly surmised then, that a Know-It-All is a person who presumes he or she "knows" everything, demands and expects, without merit, to be admired and praised by others for his or her assumed greatness, dismisses other point of views, accumulates public and personal information, and misuses the acquired knowledge with the intent to emotionally injure another person, consciously or inadvertently as well as covertly or as an affront. They may tend to see nothing as straight or even acceptable unless they bring in a touch of their genius to it.

Narcissism and Aspergers Syndrome

Narcissism and Aspergers Syndrome is often mentioned when talking about Know-It-Alls. Could either or both of these be the primary reason for a Know-It-All's pejorative Know-It-All behavior? [13] Only a Psychologist can answer that question after a psychological examination. But it is interesting to note the definition of Narcissistic Personality Disorder or NPD. Behavenet.com presents the DSM-IV & DSM-IV-TR description of NPD which states: "Individuals with this Cluster B Personality Disorder have an excessive sense of how important they are. They demand and expect to be admired and praised by others and are limited in their capacity to appreciate others' perspectives." [14] The description also presents a cautionary statement and a diagnostic criteria that must be met before someone can be diagnosed as having NPD.

James Hollis in his book "Why Good People Do Bad Things" points out that "no relationship is wholly free of ... occasional outbreaks of narcissistic self-interest ... and constitutes the ethical challenge of a relationship, namely, "to what degree can I truly love the other [person or spouse] by keeping my own needs from dominating them?"" [15] The occasional display of narcissism therefore is not the issue here; we are preoccupied with the persistent and voracious need for self adoration. This unbridled rapacious desire to be extolled in turn leads to the Know-It-All behavior, manifestations of which we will elaborate in full later in this book.

The Mayo clinic describes Asperger Syndrome, a childhood disorder that no doubt carries over into adulthood [16] since there is no cure, as "a developmental disorder that affects a person's ability to socialize and communicate effectively with others." [17] The list of symptoms include: "Engaging in one-sided, long-winded conversations, without noticing if the listener is listening or trying to change the subject ... Appearing not to understand, empathize with or be sensitive to others' feelings." Another tendency frequently associated with this syndrome and very common in the manifestation of the Know-It-All behavior is the incessant and almost impulsive need to correct others nonstop. We all welcome corrections, since that is how we learn and progress, but in this case we are not talking about appropriate and upbuilding corrections. Rather, the corrections are trivial and generally can be construed as pejorative. For example, "I saw him at 3 a.m." would be corrected to "I saw him at 3 in the morning" and other condescending, annoying and nerve wrecking corrections that alienate the Know-It-All from others. Another example may be instances in which a trivial mistake in speech may have been made, but in the overall context of the discourse or conversation and its setting the information intended is duly communicated and correctly understood by the intended audience or addressee. But the Know-It-All breaks in to correct the trivial lest humanity be doomed. The problem with an example like this one is that the all-knowing, human Auto-Correct emphasizes a slight error and makes those who may not have taken note of it know that a mistake had been made. It doesn't matter if everyone involved casts an embarrassed and dissatisfied look at them because most of such people are not even able to read other people's views of them aright.

Is technology fueling the Know-It-All behavior?

The above question can be rephrased as, "Are technological products fueling the Know-It-All behavior?" The Know-It-All behavior is nothing new, it is an inherent flaw in personality that existed before the advent of modern technology products like the cell phone, voicemail, text messages and internet based technologies such as search engines, websites, chat rooms, forums, blogs, email, social networks, etc. Hence, back then, a Know-It-All would have to spend time poring through information and different sources of knowledge that were available in libraries or bookstores. Acquiring knowledge in this manner required time and a lot of diligence which most Know-It-Alls of today probably cannot afford. The knowledge source required painstaking effort to tap; the mediums of dispensing the knowledge was few and far between, mainly orally by mouth and infrequently in writing. The audience for dispensing such knowledge was mostly workmates, loved ones and relatives in informal settings and to outsiders in closely monitored formal settings like classrooms, formal debates, public lectures and so on.

It is no surprise then, that the Know-It-All behavior is exacerbated by the ubiquity of educative, useful, useless, malicious and deceptive information through various online media, such as the Internet [18], email newsletters, online newsletters, and news alerts, etc. The accelerated pace at which such information and news are pushed to us anytime and anywhere via electronic devices, such as smart phones, cell phones, mobile access through our laptops and desktop access in the house; provides the furthering fodder for a Know-It-All. For example, a Know-It-All, who has spent countless hours soaking up such information in the luxury of his bed, all day or weekend long, will most likely arrive at work, at home, at a get-together, at a family reunion and literally offload or practically download his newly acquired knowledge on weary listeners.

But, that is to be expected. Why not? Technology has bridged the hiatus between knowledge sources that required a lot of effort to access and tap from, making them accessible with an effortless mouse click via a search engine or any of the myriads of informational websites. Furthermore, while the audience that listens to the Know-It-All and the setting where the Know-It-All dispenses their knowledge has pretty much remained the same, the knowledge delivery medium has multiplied, and it is faster and cheaper. The delivery mediums that a Know-It-All uses now includes cell phones, text messages, voicemails, chat rooms, forums, blogs, email, social networks, etc. Consequently, a Know-It-All's denigrating knowledge missile can be guided electronically and delivered to a target more precisely and frequently today than ever before. For the Know-It-All, the larger real or perceived online audience ups the stakes, the desire to shine, to be popular, to be correct always, and the desire to be praised and admired, making them even more verbally provocative, cantankerous or crabby. No wonder, the impact of the Know-It-All behavior is felt more today than ever. [19, 20]

To illustrate, imagine for a moment, that you had delivered a proposal on the environmental impact of a client's proposed new factory to your Know-It-All boss. You had requested his review and eventual approval before you can forward it to the client. After two days of inaction, it is the end of the business day on Friday and your Know-It-All boss informs you he will read it over the weekend since his family is out of town. He just ruined your weekend, because you have an idea what is going to happen. He will most likely type in the proposal's title into a search engine, locate websites on the subject, sign up in forums and blogs that discuss the subject, and basically engorge himself with whatever pertinent or irrelevant knowledge he can garner on the subject. When he walks in Monday morning and your eyes lock with his blood shot eyes, from his weekend online surfing marathon, your heart sinks. Not only do you know what that twinkle in his eyes means, but your heart sinks because the weekend surfing bonanza usually turns him into any proposal's subject matter expert, which is fine if he read your proposal thoroughly over the weekend and wants to build on it. But, no, he never reads them and when he does, your proposal almost always never meets the "latest and greatest" knowledge acquired over the weekend and will most certainly be thrashed, even with the proposal's time constraint. But then, you are happy because he could not find a suitable "online seminar." That usually spells doom for you, as he will stop the project in mid stream, attend the online seminar secretly, lecture you on the very basic knowledge he acquired and then make you attend the online seminar, even though it adds no value or additional knowledge required to complete the proposal.

How does a Know-It-All acquire and use knowledge? What is the Know-It-All's knowledge cycle? These are questions we will answer in the next chapter.

Chapter 3: How Know-It-All's Acquire and Dispense Knowledge

Let us begin by defining knowledge given that this is the primary implement of a Know-It-All. Besides, our primary concern is the usage of knowledge since a Know-It-All "knows" everything. Merriam-webster.com defines knowledge as "the range of one's information or understanding." [1] The information embodied in this range may consist of historical, geographical, mathematical, scientific, cultural, social, political and other facts accumulated academically and informally in various social settings over a large or short period of time. The information may also include experiences in life, lies fabricated from true facts, embellishments to facts, dirt hoarded from other people's failings and weaknesses, intimate secrets entrusted in confidence, unfounded gossip bandied by close associates, malicious prejudice fomented from ignorance and so forth.

The anatomy of a Know-It-All's knowledge

A Know-It-All dispenses information in a verbal conversation using words spoken or written. The conversation can take place face to face or electronically or online. The knowledge is dispensed as a combination of words to convey information. The problem with Know-It-Alls stem from the manner in which the words are arranged and dispensed.

To illustrate, let us describe a typical weapon such as a gun. A gun fires a bullet. The bullet consists of an outer casing that houses the bullet propellant, typically gunpowder. A bullet also contains a projectile at the tip, as well as other parts. For the purposes of our illustration, let us imagine that words are like gunpowder, knowledge the bullet and the medium through which the knowledge is dispensed the gun itself. As we all know, guns are carried by law enforcement officials as a deterrent and for self defense if necessary. On the other hand, an armed robber carries a gun to intimidate, humiliate and cause bodily harm if necessary. The difference in the reason the two groups of individuals carry guns exemplifies the difference between a knowledgeable person and a Know-It-All. For a knowledgeable person, knowledge is used to inform and upbuild others in a dignified and respectful manner. It leaves the audience or listeners refreshed and ready for another session. For a Know-It-All, knowledge is like a bullet with carefully concealed gunpowder, words. It is used to intimidate, humiliate, impress, seek praise, disparage and self aggrandize. The medium, just like a gun, used to dispense or "fire" the "knowledge bullets" is usually their mouth verbally or other electronic mediums like a cell phone, voicemail, text messages or online mediums like chat rooms, forums, blogs, email, social networks, etc. [6] This much we can deduce from just the definition of a Know-It-All. Much later in this chapter we will discuss the medium and setting in more details and later in the book we will discuss the impact of the "knowledge bullets."

With the above apt, vivid and visual illustration, now we can understand the reason we see dramatic responses to a simple question such as "What do you do for a living?" at a social gathering. A knowledgeable person will respectfully respond; cede ground to others to contribute and respond respectfully to appropriate length, to questions asked about their professional lives. But not so for Know-It-Alls! It is an invitation to load their "knowledge bullets" and take center stage, ready to take pot shots at their audience, to boast, elevate self, lecture the audience, show how great they are as well as how popular they are at work and put down their audience with belittling questions or condescending answers to questions. When we watch news clips of an armed bandit taking pot shots at people, what do people do in general? They run for cover, right? Well, guess what the Know-It-All's audience will most likely do? It is in similar awkward situations that guests suddenly remember a quick but "important" call to make, gulp down their wine, excuse themselves and head out to refill or simply hurry to the safety of the restroom. Some even wave to an imaginary friend at the other end of the room and run for cover!

The primary conversation characteristics of a Know-It-All

A Know-It-All dispenses knowledge in a verbal conversation using spoken or written words as described earlier in this chapter. Conversation is the interchange of thoughts and information between persons. [2] Today, we can add electronic and online conversations [3] to this definition as this is increasingly becoming a mode of conversation or interchange of information, if not a preferred mode of conversation for some people. The perceived anonymity in this mode of conversation, perceived because no online or electronic conversation is anonymous or secret or truly private, engenders or emboldens ordinarily taciturn persons to become talkative virtually speaking. You may have encountered such people in the comments sections of some Internet news pages or blogs. They use the imagined anonymity of the Internet to spew outrageous texts and tend to teach everyone else on the forum everything from constitution to history, from healthcare to economics.

Elaborating on the illustration used earlier, it is logical to conclude that when an armed bandit is taking pot shots at passersby, anybody hit by the bullet will be injured, except of course, those protected by a bulletproof vest. Equally, Know-It-Alls' pot shots cause emotional injury to anybody hit by their "knowledge bullets" unless they are protected with the knowledge of how to deal with a Know-It-All. We will discuss these emotional effects in detail much later in this book. But for now let us examine the characteristics of a Know-It-All's conversation and gain insight into some ways the Know-It-All behavior is manifested.

Why can we classify a Know-It-All's conversation as verbally abusive? "Verbal abuse defines people in some negative way, and it creates emotional pain and mental anguish... Any statement that tells you ... what you think, feel or want, is defining you and is, therefore, abusive." [4] Someone who denigrates or argues against other people's points of view, opinions, personal preferences and so on can be classified as verbally abusive. [5, 6] These definitions may come as a surprise to some Know-It-Alls, who probably think they are trying to help out, or enlighten their audience or prevent something bad from happening to their listener or audience. Some Know-It-Alls may mentally justify the verbally abusive manifestation of their knowledge as being inline with the well worn cliché "No pain no gain!" So then, they erroneously think that for their audience to gain, their audience should pay its mental penance for lacking the dispensed knowledge. They make their audience pay by delivering emotional pain via their carefully aimed or staccato "knowledge bullet." The point is that, the impact of a Know-It-All's "knowledge bullet" can, in varying levels, cause "emotional pain and mental anguish."

What else in the conversation of a Know-It-All can be related to verbal abuse? Bullying! Bullying is a "continual ... verbal or emotional methods of intimidation by an individual or group. ...that makes you feel angry, hurt and upset." [7] Bullying is most often mistakenly or equivocally associated with physical belligerence or physical manhandling of sorts, but that is far from the truth, verbal bullying [8] can be just as detrimental in causing "emotional pain and mental anguish". As we saw earlier, a Know-It-All manifests the Know-It-All behavior by intimidating his audience or listener with "knowledge bullets" carefully aimed and fired or fired in a staccato fashion, with the sole purpose of humiliating [9], eliciting angry and hurt feelings. Today, the medium through which the bullying is delivered is no longer only through the mouth, but has extended to electronic medium like voicemail, cell phones, and text messages as well as a prevalent online medium such as chat rooms, forums, blogs, email, social networks, etc.

Verbal aggression or abuse as manifested in a Know-It-All's conversation is also strongly linked with a domineering attitude. [10] Since the Know-It-All behavior is usually exhibited verbally in conversations, the domineering attitude manifests in negative challenges, braggadocio and denigrating speech. [10] It is not surprising then that men [and women] who dominate conversations as they hatch out knowledge and fabricate "knowledge bullets", are generally disliked universally. [11]

Debates and arguments can sometimes be healthy, if engaged in a friendly and organized manner, but a Know-It-All usually will cross the line in other to win or dominate the debate or argument at all cost. The rules of conversation include speaking very clearly, not dominating the conversation, allowing others to express their opinions completely without interrupting them; not criticizing people behind their backs; sticking to the subject at hand, not hijacking the conversation to talk or educate or lecture others about ourselves, keeping our temper under check, remembering and using peoples' names in a dignifying manner and being an empathic listener. [12] For a Know-It-All these conversation rules can be difficult to abide with.

One of the observed manifestations of the Know-It-All behavior when the above rules of conversation are not followed can be seen when a participant in the conversation shifts from being an equal participant in the conversation to a Know-It-All. The conversation in turn shifts into a speech or lecture, delivered by the Know-It-All, before his captive audience. [13]

It is evident that a Know-It-All's conversation includes various characteristics that are manifestations of the Know-It-All behavior such verbal abuse, bulling, domineering attitude and lots more. We will enumerate other manifestations of the Know-It-All behavior and elaborate on these manifestations in more details later in the book. From this point forward, we will also use the word victim interchangeably with the person receiving the brunt of the Know-It-All behavior.

The Know-It-All's verbal and non-verbal communication medium of disseminating knowledge

The communication medium used by Know-It-Alls to disseminate their knowledge depends on the setting. The primary medium of dissemination is usually through the mouth, verbally or vocally as was discussed in the previous section and this is amenable in social settings where face to face conversation takes place. Non-verbal, non-electronic and non-online mediums include handwritten notes, letters and even writing boards be they blackboards or whiteboards.

One will probably think it will be difficult for Know-It-Alls to dispense their "knowledge bullets" in a letter or on a writing board. These are actually situations where Know-It-Alls become really creative, since it enables their hurtful, condescending and denigrating words to be etched, as it were, with ink on to the writing paper, bolded and underlined so the victim does not miss the words. It is almost as if their pen has turned into a dagger, stabbing the words onto the pages or their chalks or markers have turned into knives cutting into the writing board. This is for what purpose, though? The purpose is so their vitriolic words like little pockets or concentrations of gunpowder will explode when they are read and get burned onto the victim's brain indelibly, thereby causing as much emotional harm as possible. Do you recall ever seeing someone cry after reading a letter of this kind? Later in this book, we will discuss in detail the effects of a Know-It-All's behavior on their victim.

The truth of the matter is that no matter how a "knowledge bullet" is fired, most people will recognize it for what it is, a malicious intent by a Know-It-All to degrade or disparage. But then, what do law enforcement officials worldwide sometimes use to "control" crowds? They have guns with bullets, but they don't use those to "control" crowds. They sometimes use rubber pellets. Rubber pellets don't cause a lot of harm, but they sting and help keep the crowd or riot in check or under "control". Don't you think a Know-It-All would love those? After all, it can be fired, it will not kill, but it will sting and most importantly "control" a victim. Let us call this addition to a Know-It-All's arsenal "knowledge pellet."

What are "knowledge pellets" and how do Know-It-Alls use them? Well, "knowledge pellets" are those subtle but malicious non-verbal one-way conversations that Know-It-Alls have with their victim or a target; a person who needs to be tutored on how important or how great they are. Although the conversation is non-verbal, it can be considered a conversation since information, albeit in an encoded and one-way fashion, is being interchanged with the victim. The word interchange is appropriate since the victim responds to the communication. Such non-verbal communication serves the same purpose that rubber pellets serve; to control the victim without words and we will discuss this in detail later in the book. Let us consider just a few of the malicious non-verbal one-way conversations that Know-It-Alls have with their victim.

Facial expression is one of them and it could be in the form of a frown, a furrowed forehead, a sneer, a lip smack and so forth. All these facial expressions are used to convey disdain and disapproval designed to sting and to gradually sap the self confidence of the victim. The eyes are used to fire "knowledge pellets", perhaps to actualize the well worn cliché "if eyes could kill." The eyes are used to convey a condescending air of superiority designed to make the victim cower or they could be just plain hostile like daggers! The eyes could also be used to exclude [6] the victim. To exclude the victim, the Know-It-All makes eye contact with everyone in a group setting except the victim, thereby conveying to the victim that he or she is too inconsequential to be recognized or that he or she don't exist [14] or that the victim is not worth being accorded dignity by the "royal highness" Mr. or Mrs. or Miss Know-It-All!

The tone of voice is another useful "knowledge pellet", perhaps used more often in relationships between a Know-It-All and a victim or perhaps between two Know-It-Alls. The tone of voice could be jeering, or perhaps adjusted to belt out mock humility or just plain mock their victim. This is an indirect way of conveying disdain. The tone of voice could be harsh also, to convey instant disapproval. The tone and pitch of laughter, whether civil, raucous or derisive can be used to exert influence or control [15] over a victim, thereby conveying approval or disapproval. The tone of voice combined with words could also be used to make the victim feel excluded. In other words, although Know-It-Alls are not directing their words at their victim who is standing next to them, they make references to the victim as if they were not standing there or as if they are some "absentee third party" to the conversation.

Have you given gifts in the past, perhaps to show someone how much you cared about them? That is not so for some Know-It-Alls. For such Know-It-Alls a gift has to be "meaningful". That is another way of saying, "Of what use is a gift if it cannot fire a silent message or "knowledge pellet"?" For such Know-It-Alls, a gift is a "knowledge pellet" disguised thoroughly, but nonetheless just as insulting and annoying. Here are examples of such gifts. You get a cookbook as a gift, but the real message is; your cooking is bland, read up some recipes please! You get a dictionary as a gift, but the real message is; your spelling leaves much to be desired, you could do with a lot of practice. You get an exercise DVD or Blu-ray Disc for a gift, the not so indirect message is; you could look better if you shed a few pounds or perhaps they will give the deliberate gift of a smaller dress or shirt size to drive the point home. How about the neighbor in the apartment downstairs, who gives you the gift of a door mat that says; "Silence is Golden?" But the real message is; your kids are too loud, we could have more peace here if they were quieter!

Countering is also another "knowledge pellet" which is used verbally though sometimes non-verbally, but the real impact is in the unsaid. "Countering is verbal [and non-verbal] opposition that negates the other's opinions, feelings, and beliefs." [14] Have you ever met or talked with someone who always and constantly has an opposing view or opinion for every idea, thought or opinion you express? It does not matter what the subject or time of day it is, he or she will counter you. And yes, his or her opinion or view had to have an edge over yours, a typical one-up. Here is the part that "kills" you. You have heard this particular Know-It-All express similar views to what you just expressed, in the past, to someone else, but yet, he or she just countered and negated what you said. What is the point or "knowledge pellet" being fired here by the Know-It-All? Well, obviously, the Know-It-All has to be smarter than you, they have to be the one "hatching out" the knowledge you need, they are on center stage not you, they hand out and you receive, they have to have the last word. Furthermore, why are you not praising and admiring the Know-It-All's brilliance? That is your expected role as a Know-It-All's "friend" and "confidant." Well, that is probably why we spring a headache around Know-It-Alls who counter us all the time, that is, until we run for cover.

Here is a non-verbal version of the countering one-up scenario. Your Know-It-All neighbor mows his lawn at least twice a week to make your side of the lot looks weedy, even when you mow your lawn weekly. Then, when you start mowing yours twice a week, your Know-It-All neighbor starts to more his thrice a week! Or he washes his car daily and then makes sure to park, almost always, next to yours; washed a week ago. Then there are the Know-It-All workmates, the ones you share a cube with and they deliberately keep their desktop spick-and-span to accentuate your somewhat not too tidy desktop. You know it is deliberate because they have all their junk stashed away haphazardly out of sight in their drawers and under their desk.

The Know-It-All's electronic and online communication medium of disseminating knowledge

Though electronic and online communication mediums are listed as secondary here, it probably is the primary way of disseminating hurtful words for some Know-It-Alls who are computer savvy and it is becoming more popular by the day as electronic means of communication and the internet becomes ubiquitous. There is no doubt that technology is empowering a new breed of verbal abusers, [17] even if the verbal abuse is delivered; disguised as knowledge interchange. Do you know a Know-It-All friend, or Know-It-All workmate or Know-It-All relative who just discovered the internet or chat rooms or social networks or text messages or instant messages and the world has suffered ever since? Does your Know-It-All boss belong to an online forum and for that reason all key decisions has to be made based on what "the forum" suggests is doable? Or, all of your team's dirty linen and confidential matters are first aired in "the forum" and then "they", that is, your boss and "the forum" will decide what is best for you non-forum inferiors! And typically, as sometimes occurs in such situations, all common sense previously in use by your team to solve certain problems goes out the window against your team's advice and practical wisdom. The problem is not the internet based technologies or the forum. These technologies and the forum are meant to complement our work and not supplant them.

But what is the lure? Why do Know-It-Alls love electronic and online medium of disseminating their so-called knowledge. To answer that question with an illustration let us extend the "knowledge bullet" and "knowledge pellet" metaphor that gyrates on ballistics. Armies have and routinely still use missiles in wars. These missiles are generally fired from a location that is unknown to the target. The person or unit firing the missile may have the coordinates and general location of their target. Other than that, there is no direct physical or direct visual contact with the target. The missile is pretty much like a bigger bullet, loaded with explosives of sorts. Furthermore, today's missiles are intelligent and guided in their trajectory until they hit their target.

Electronic and online communication technologies share some similarities with a guided missile system. There is no direct physical or direct visual contact between a person sending a message or conversing and the target. Think of all the possibilities this provides for Know-It-Alls intent on hurting with a payload of disparaging words. In this scenario, the wireless telecommunication network or the internet network becomes the guided path for their "knowledge eMissile" loaded with offensive knowledge. The "knowledge eMissile" is fired with the click of a mouse and it is guided with precision to an exact coordinate of their victim, that is, their cell phone number or email address or online profile or as a forum posting or as a chat response or a blog response. For the Know-It-All, the words "post" and "submit", possibly, becomes synonymous with "fire" or "trigger" or "detonate" and who knows what else!

The perceived anonymity of the mouse click, that activates the "post" and "submit" buttons, [although "trigger" buttons would sound better for a Know-It-All], that in turn fires off the message, is the biggest lure. Why? This is because that allows the Know-It-All to assemble a no holds barred "knowledge eMissile." Sure, a web cam can provide visuals, but that will default to a verbal conversation that negates anonymity would it not? Another lure is the speed [17] at which the "knowledge eMissile" arrives at its target, almost at the blink of an eye. There is no need to dress up and drive over for a face to face conversation. The cost of sending such a message is a minuscule fraction of the cost of effecting a face to face conversation. Furthermore, the Know-It-All has more time to think over his words without compunction, assemble explosive and denigrating words, spell check them before launching the "knowledge eMissile." Today, words like e-bully [18] or even e-harasser are associated with people who intimidate, harass, denigrate and bully with words. These people include Know-It-Alls who use words, assembled as knowledge, in a similar manner. Let us examine in more detail the electronic and online medium, and especially the way Know-It-Alls use them to launch and guide their "knowledge eMissile" to victims.

Before the advent of cell phones most people had phones at home and at work. Most personal calls were made at home after work. Today, with the availability of cell phones and their accessibility financially, it has grown into one of the most used modes of conversation on a daily basis. A cell phone owner can literally keep in touch from anywhere, almost twenty four hours a day, with anybody who has a phone. The enabling and handy tools in a cell phone empower Know-It-Alls. For example, Know-It-Alls do not have to assemble a captive audience in any one physical location and regale them with their daily achievements, how popular they suddenly became at work, how they want to resign and how their boss and the company is begging them to stay, how "all" the women at work want them even though they are married men and so forth. They can connect everyone in their audience in a conference call and fire away a few "knowledge eMissiles."

Before the advent of cell phones, Know-It-Alls could at least be cornered more easily in a conversation and you could point out a few weak points or unsubstantiated points in the constituents of their argument or reasoning. Today, Know-It-Alls can easily turn on the speaker phone on their cell phone and perform a quick web search on the internet while listening to you and talking. This specific ability is not only empowering but intoxicating, because it adds to their arsenal and makes them almost invincible in arguments that require facts to prove a point. It also adds a virtual extension to the Know-It-All's mental capabilities, making the Know-It-All appear larger than life. Another use of the speaker phone by Know-It-Alls is to humiliate an unsuspecting victim on the other side, who is possibly conversing in confidence, thinking they are on a one-on-one conversation, not realizing that for a Know-It-All there is more shine and popularity in numbers. There has to be an audience in other to maximize the shine and feed the "expectation" of a Know-It-All's admirers.

With the advent of cell phone technologies; came voice mails. A voice mail can be saved, forwarded or even transcribed into text with the press of a button. For Know-It-Alls, this is the perfect place to leave "knowledge eMissile", perhaps booby trapped to ensure you listen to the whole message, by prefacing it with "kind" words. They could call back several times to leave messages, especially if the intent is to win some obscure argument or prove a cheap point or even worse, to grind in a grudge. A voice mail can also be used in reverse by Know-It-Alls. They can forward a victim's intimate and private message sent to them to virtually anybody, if that can further their course or agenda.

Today, the average U.S. cell phone subscriber makes fewer voice calls in comparison with the number of text messages sent. [19] Thousands of text messages are exchanged monthly by most teenagers. This phenomenon is also true worldwide. Just like voicemails, Know-It-Alls can forward a victim's intimate and private text message sent to them to virtually anybody. Now imagine a victim who had engaged in sexting with a

Know-It-All intent on winning an argument or proving how popular he is and how all the girls in school want him! Disastrous! But then, of what use will text messaging be if it cannot be used to broadcast how smart, how funny and how intelligent the Know-It-All is? It will not serve their self-seeking purpose, right? Hence, a denigrating message to a victim can be broadcast simultaneously to the victim and to the Know-It-All's cronies with the press of a button.

Worldwide, 247 billion emails are sent everyday, that is, almost 2.8 million emails per second! [20] The numbers attest to the popularity of email as a medium of communication, although text messages surpass this number by an order of magnitude. Businesses today rely on email to communicate internally and externally to other businesses. That also means that Know-It-Alls can hide behind the zillions of emails flying back and forth, on corporate and private networks, and unleash a few salvos of their "knowledge eMissiles". After all, that conforms to the well worn cliché "there is safety in numbers." For such Know-It-Alls, emails also have a multiplicity of usage settings. Emails can be fired from work, from their cell phone, from their laptop or from a home computer. For some Know-It-Alls, composing an email is a pleasure, because not only do they have spell checkers to check the exactness of words but they can easily locate explosive [17] and shrapnel-like words that will do the most damage to their victim when their payload is delivered.

Know-It-Alls additionally are capable of highlighting, bolding; underlining and enlarging the explosive, scathing and shrapnel-like words and phrases in their email to maximize impact, abuse, [21] humiliation and intimidation of their victim. But then, if only the victim received the email, how does that increase the

Know-It-All's shine or popularity? Often Know-It-Alls don't maintain their "popularity" by sending an email to one person. That is where the "cc" or carbon copy comes in handy. Such Know-It-Alls have to copy their admirers and sycophants, so they too can partake of the Know-It-All's moment of glory. If the email is directed to the Know-It-All's boss, they cannot copy their cronies. Is there a way for such Know-It-Alls to "permit" their admirers to see how smart they are and how they "educate" their boss? Yes there is! They will use the "bcc" blind carbon copy. Another sphere of email usage where some Know-It-Alls shine is correcting the grammatical errors [29, 30] in emails they receive and responding back with "Reply All." Why not? A Know-It-All may ask, explaining that the response was aimed at helping team members improve their grammar, so they don't make the same mistakes like the victim. And well, additionally, it helps Know-It-Alls think they are establishing themselves as the go-to-grammar-expert of the team. You know; the grammar expert the whole team admires and looks up to! Guesstimating from the share number of emails exchanged daily, it will not be far fetched to say that the most damaging "knowledge eMissiles" sent by Know-It-Alls are via emails at work, at home and mobile, while up and about on their cell phones and laptops.

Forums are online virtual places, where people who share similar interests gather to exchange ideas, discuss and answer questions of mutual interest, and interact generally. [26] These interests could be in any field or endeavor. Contributions to the discussion are made in the form of postings, that is, a contributor's comment is saved on the host computer and presented to members for viewing as part of the forum goings-on. Responses to posts do not have to be immediate; hence, they can be posted minutes, hours or days later. If you can already see the lure for Know-It-Alls, you are a not alone. The fact that there is a readymade audience, ready to recognize their brilliance and admire them is one lure. Camouflaged as part of the forum activities, some Know-It-Alls can target a victim with subterfuge and fire their "knowledge eMissiles." The perceived large audience in a forum further ups the ante for Know-It-Alls, making them exhibit the Know-It-All behavior in all its ramifications. It is in these forums that Know-It-Alls will say things that they will not ordinarily say in a face to face conversation. [21] In other words, caution is thrown to the wind and "knowledge eMissiles" are fired more easily at a victim.

Chat rooms share basically the same principles as a forum. [26] One of the differences is that the chat or conversation or information exchange happens in real time, that is, the information sent by each participant is seen almost instantly. Furthermore, while the transcript of the chat can be stored and published later, it is not generally publicly available to persons outside the virtual chat room. Chat rooms provide the preying ground for quick witted Know-It-Alls to identify a victim and revile them with incessant grammatical corrections [25] and or attempts to deride the victim's opinions and supplant it with theirs.

Social networking websites allow members to own their own pages or websites where they can post profiles of themselves and their interests. However, these websites also provide emails, forums and chat rooms that allow members to interact and those are what Know-It-Alls use mostly on these social network websites. [22, 27] The young girl who committed suicide as a consequence of messages she received on a popular social networking website demonstrates the use of electronic and online mediums as a new anonymous attack medium [23] which some naively think is really anonymous. Some Know-It-Alls arm themselves with the information gleaned from their victim's posted profile, and then use those in the preparation of their "knowledge eMissiles." Later we will discuss how Know-It-Alls use fake profile pages in social networking websites.

The conversational settings where Know-It-Alls disseminate knowledge

Conversational settings are places where the interaction or exchange of words or information takes place. The exchange may be spontaneous or delayed as we discussed earlier. Some of these settings have been discussed in the previous section, namely chat rooms, forums and social networks.

Other conversational settings include social gatherings where friends, relatives and even strangers gather for a social event. In such settings, some Know-It-Alls would try to draw attention to themselves; or use the opportunity to fire a few salvos at their victim tucked away innocently in the audience. This is the type of setting where a Know-It-All uncle or aunt or even a parent would take it upon themselves to lecture the audience, talking to the audience in a condescending disrespectful manner. By the time the Know-It-All is done talking, friends and strangers are privy to the intimate and embarrassing details of a selected number of victims. In this setting, often Know-It-Alls will deliberately ignite a simple tête-à-tête into a debate with invectives designed to make them shine, prove others wrong [28] or increase their popularity and could become completely adamant in the face of reasoning. For Know-

It-Alls who love correcting [24] others in other to shine, or to humiliate and expose others; this is a perfect setting.

Friends and or Family hanging out in their vehicles, boats, bars, restaurants or wherever is another setting where Know-It-Alls like to hijack the conversation. Know-It-Alls get real loud and take control as a way of ensuring that all attention is centered on them. This is the kind of setting where most of the verbal and non-verbal disseminating of knowledge takes place. In this setting "knowledge bullets" and "knowledge pellets" are used with dexterity.

In literature reviewed, the workplace continues to be the most written about setting where Know-It-Alls hold sway. This is probably because the number of Know-It-Alls per employee is bound to be higher than in any other setting, except one setting we will discuss shortly. Another reason for the popularity in literature could be because there are more recorded incidents where the Know-It-All behavior was manifested as workplace harassment, verbal abuse, bullying, sabotage and other manifestations of the Know-It-All behavior. The ubiquity of the Know-It-All behavior in the workplace could as well be because the workplace setting indirectly engenders such behavior. Here is why. In the workplace, the audience could potentially be huge both virtually and face to face, and since Know-It-Alls need to be admired or shine in the throng of congregated workmates it becomes irresistible to them. Another reason could be because, by its very nature, the workplace is a place that fosters and nurtures intellectual growth and healthy competition. This is true in all workplaces, be they work places where the task is manual and repetitive or a high tech workplace.

Take for example, a team of five loaders who load furniture, from a warehouse the size of two football fields, into endless line of trucks. Clearly, it requires a lot of manual dexterity to operate the machinery safely and load the trucks safely. But it also requires a lot of mental capacity to load the trucks fast enough, in an orderly manner and possibly meet the daily quotas. Some Know-It-Alls in a team like this will figure out a way to outshine the rest of the team and disparage their team members before their manager, in attempt to be admired by the manager. That brings us to another point. Oftentimes, Know-It-Alls will do what ever it takes to shine in front of their managers or bosses including challenging other employees or the boss on trivial stuff, becoming hold outs in team meetings where crucial decisions need to be made. Perhaps, arguing blindly about a trivial detail that adds nothing to the big picture, discarding other teammate's opinions and views. [31] The reverse is also true in these settings, where a boss is the Know-It-All who laces managerial instruction with abusive speech [32], humiliating innuendos and overtures. The Know-It-All boss fires "knowledge bullets" with abandon, stifles creative expressions or claims them to a point where the Know-It-All boss' subordinates begin to wonder if the Know-It-All boss was competing with them.

The workplace further provides other avenues that can stir up the Know-It-All behavior in a Know-It-All employee or Know-It-All boss. These include online meetings, online presentations, phone conferences, team meetings, one-on-one meetings, company get-togethers, team excursions, team group lunch, etc. In all these avenues, the audience is a prime target for a Know-It-All to show off. Take online presentations for example, sometimes you will have Know-It-All employees or

Know-It-All bosses making these presentations. For some Webster Know-It-Alls such a presentation invariably starts smoothly, and then by the time they get to slide 3 of 30 in a one-hour presentation they deviate. Such Know-It-Alls pick one point on slide 3 and then veering off in a tangent, they begin to expound on the sometimes trivial details. The idea in their "side-bar" lecture, they state loudly for all to hear, is to make sure that "every one is on the same page", whereas the deviation most often is self serving; to show how smart and how deep and knowledgeable they are on the subject. Or it could be a retaliation to expose a victim attending the meeting as being ignorant and unintelligent. Or that the presentation made by the victim during the last online meeting is not at par with their "great presentation." By the time they swerve off course a few times, it is almost an hour and they are yet to get to slide 15. Well, you can guess how the rest of the 15 slides will go.

Then, you could also have a Clavin making the presentation. Obsessed with trying to impress, a Clavin Know-It-All will pull all kinds of gimmicks to make attendees sound dumb or to make attendees appreciate his or her "greatness." Sometimes a condescending question and answer session is used to prop up the intoned air of superiority. In this scenario, a Clavin Know-It-All will read a line from the slide, for example, that says: "A project team is made up of team members." Then, in a disdainful and derisive manner the Clavin Know-It-All will ask: "Joseph! Is a project team made up of team members?" Superficially, this is a trivial question and humility demands that the question be answered to honor the presenter at the very least. But what is the actual "knowledge pellet" being fired by the Clavin Know-It-All with this inconsequential question?

The Clavin Know-It-All could be simply trying to confirm if the victim is still on the call or to see if they are paying attention and if not, fire off a more offensive "knowledge bullet" to humiliate the victim for not paying attention to the ongoing "great presentation."

Radio and television is another setting where a Know-It-All host [33] or guest can display the Know-It-All behavior. Sometimes a simple banter between host and guest is hijacked by the Know-It-All and it turns into a lecture to educate the host or guest and the myriads of viewers or listeners. Like in most settings where there is a large audience, the stake is high for Know-It-Alls during radio and television interviews. So, in other to keep the shine and admirers, such Know-It-Alls will discard or reject every sound view or opinion offered and promote their view or opinion even when it is illogical and flawed in the court of public opinion and common sense. Oh yes, usually, there is an angle and depth of reasoning, that "privileged and gifted" people like the Know-It-All have, which others don't see or are not capable of comprehending. That, they claim is the reason for being inflexible.

Home is the primary battle ground for most Know-It-Alls. This is where the Know-It-All behavior is most observable. Why? Remember all those corporate Know-It-Alls from the workplace? Well, they have to go home at the end of the day, will they not? Guess who takes the brunt of their bruised egos from work? Their family members have to put up with their behavior. Sometimes it is just the Know-It-All and a mate. In this setting, Know-It-Alls have more in their knowledge arsenal, namely, the personal flaws, the weaknesses, the needs, the intimate secrets and the trusting nature of family members. To some Know-It-Alls in this setting, any of those could be used against the victim to maintain supremacy in family relations.

The setting in a school is similar to that in radio and television, large audiences, patient listeners and a bounteous number of possible victims within reach. The Know-It-All teacher or the Know-It-All student generally hides their nefarious intentions better in these settings. Hence, in a slip of tongue when a teacher mispronounces or misspells a word, the Know-It-All student sees the setting as the perfect opportunity to humiliate the teacher, perhaps in retaliation for a perceived poor grade received. Why not? The Know-It-All student may self-righteously ask; after all, the classroom is a place where everyone learns, and besides, the teacher is not perfect, the teacher should be glad for the help rendered by being corrected in front of the class! The reverse is also true, where a Know-It-All teacher victimizes select students in the name of helping them "academically." This is the setting where Know-It-All students wreck the most havoc with text messages and sexting.

The audience of a Know-It-All

Regardless of the setting or the type of conversation, a Know-It-All must have an audience to converse with and impress with their "great knowledge." Without an audience to listen to them, no matter how briefly, the Know-It-All cannot exhibit the Know-It-All behavior. Who then constitute the Know-It-All's audience? They run the gamut and include: wives, husbands, children, sons, daughters, fathers, mothers, cousins, uncles, aunts, workmates, employees, bosses, teachers, students, radio and television audiences and so forth.

The Know-It-All's knowledge cycle

In this chapter we defined knowledge which is the main implement of Know-It-Alls. We described what constitutes knowledge for a Know-It-All and how Know-It-Alls used them in conversations. We also defined what a conversation is and how conversations with Know-It-Alls take place through verbal or non-verbal, electronic and online mediums. Finally, we talked about the settings where Know-It-Alls disseminate their knowledge. All these constitute the knowledge cycle of Know-It-Alls, that is, knowledge acquisition, selecting the medium of dissemination, choosing a setting, discerning the appropriate audience and finally disseminating their pejorative knowledge like a "knowledge bullet".

Chapter 4: Types of Know-It-All

Earlier we defined a Know-It-All as a person who presumes he or she "knows" everything, demands and expects, without merit, to be admired and praised by others for his or her greatness, dismisses other point of views, accumulates public and personal information, and misuses the acquired knowledge with the intent to emotionally injure another person, consciously or inadvertently as well as covertly or as an affront. The Know-It-All behavior is observed and felt by their victims in the settings described in the last chapter. Hence, the classification of Know-It-Alls into types will generally tend to reflect the settings where the behavior is observed and or the relationship the Know-It-All has with the victim. The types of Know-It-All described below are blends or montages or composites derived from literature, articles, forum postings, blogs, websites, dictionaries, encyclopedias, personal experiences, people's experiences, etc. Let us examine a few types of Know-It-All.

The Know-It-All Backseat Driver

A backseat driver, in our case for a vehicle, is "an automobile passenger who offers the driver unsolicited advice, warnings, criticism, etc., esp[ecially] from the backseat." [1] Why would the passenger be offering unsolicited advice, especially when there is no immediate danger to the driver or the occupants or the vehicle? You guessed correctly, because the passenger is a Know-It-All backseat driver. Know-It-All backseat drivers usually give the impression that they are "experts" in driving skills, habits and very knowledgeable in highway driving codes. Oh, lest you forget, their uncle works for the DOT [Department of Transport] and keeps them abreast, "daily", of changes in DOT highway codes!

Know-It-All backseat drivers are usually normal and friendly until their victim cranks up the engine. Then it is almost as if they switch to a different mental mode. Their first vocalized observation may include the windshield being a safety hazard because it is not spic-span to their "standard" or may be the windows of the vehicle are too tinted in their "opinion" or that the windows have too much smear on them. By the time the victim changes gears and rolls onto the street, the Know-It-All backseat driver transforms into an "overwrought, twitchy, [nervous] ... frazzled, fidgety passenger" [2] who stops shot of wresting the steering wheel from the victim; to show them how to drive! If Know-It-All backseat drivers only felt nervous and left it at that, it would not be so bad. But No! They have to vocalize all the required actions needed to keep the vehicle "safe" and in "compliance" with highway codes. They will let you know when the light turns green, tell you when to stop to avoid driving through the red light, remind you of the posted speed limit as you drive past the speed limit signs, remind you of each turn as you drive to your mother's house, interpret the objects that appear in your side mirrors so you can focus on driving! Have you ever seen a Know-It-All backseat driver's head bobbing from side to side as you drive? No, they are not dozing off. As your vehicle speed "enforcement" passenger; your speed is being monitored by the Know-It-All backseat driver.

The Know-It-All Armchair Quarterback

An armchair quarterback, in our case for any sporting event or game, is a "viewer who criticizes conduct of games: somebody who is certain that he or she can make better calls than the coaches or players while watching a competitive sport on television." [3] Naturally, we should expect Know-It-All armchair quarterbacks to be hypercritical or to make "better" calls than those engaged in the actual activity. Why will they not make "better" calls when they are seated on expensive leather sofas, frothy beer in hand, jaws grinding away at their favorite pepper laced hotdog and watching the game on a 60-inch ultra color LCD television? What else is needed to make "better" calls? Join the players, in the snow patched field, in sub zero temperature?

This is not to say that Know-It-All armchair quarterbacks do not understand the sport they are commenting on or criticizing. Understanding a sport and having a general idea of how the sports statistics relate to the actual play should be enough to hold an engaging relaxing conversation with friends and family watching the sporting event. However, for Know-It-All armchair quarterbacks the itch for self admiration, the tendency to let everyone think they know more about the sport than everyone else in the room usually overrides their sense of modesty. When this sense of modesty is overridden, that is when "thrash talk" begins and sometimes the visiting friends and family become the targets for the disparaging, negative and belittling remarks. This does not mean that all "thrash talk" is bad, but some can lead to confrontational showdowns with Know-It-All armchair quarterbacks, where opinions and statistics get stretched or exaggerated out of proportion.

Ordinarily, you will think that Know-It-All armchair quarterbacks are talking from experience, perhaps from having participated physically or practically in the sport in the past. No, most of them have never "really" played the sport they are criticizing, although they know the rules and understand the sport. But, why should we expect them to have played the sport in the past? They already "know" the sport! That is why they are Know-It-All armchair quarterbacks for crying out loud.

The Know-It-All Co-worker

Have you worked with a Know-It-All co-worker who constantly interrupted you, sometimes, more times than you care to be bothered in the course of a work day? Have you ever caught your Know-It-All co-worker snooping around your email, drawers or handbag or personal belongings? How else can the Know-It-All co-worker gather dirt against you? Then, there are the endless "little" prying questions Know-It-All co-workers ask, that really have nothing to do with the job and come across as insensitive. It is almost as if the Know-It-All co-worker is on an information gathering session. Of course, you can deal with all that. But then, the Know-It-All co-worker always seems to have a never-ending list of opinions, tips and unsolicited advice, offered in a condescending manner, while your views and opinions are discarded between breaths. Often these tips and advice about how you should do your job are completely unrelated to the kind of job the Know-It-All co-worker does. Even more annoying is the fact that some of those tips have been painfully incorrect in the past, but the Know-It-All co-worker quickly levels the blame on how you executed the tip.

In team meetings, often Know-It-All co-workers will purposefully answer questions directed at you so they can assert their opinions quickly and dismiss or counter yours later. They will cut you off in mid sentence and finish the sentence for you. Of course, they "know" exactly what you were thinking and so they unabashedly "helped" you out. When they are not cutting you off in mid sentence they are obsessed with correcting grammatical errors and other trivial details that do nothing more than interrupt conversation. Did you expect the Know-It-All co-worker not to shine while trying to impress the boss who is moderating the meeting? Remember that wherever there is an audience and a conversation going on, Know-It-Alls will tend to display the Know-It-All behavior.

The Know-It-All Employee

Some Know-It-All employees for unexplained reasons seem to single out their boss and become an enigma that is impossible to resolve. They will obstinately hold up decisions in a meeting with lop-sided and close minded arguments that cannot be substantiated. Ideas or instructions from the boss that conflict with their strongly entrenched opinions are immediately criticized and torn down with much ado. When the boss asks for their opinion or comment or view point, they will typically see that as an opportunity to dominate the conversation and expound their "brilliance" to the rest of the "inferior" team members and the "not too smart" boss. For such Know-It-All employees a smart boss in their opinion does not ask for the view point of underlings. The "brilliance" being expounded by such Know-It-All employees most often is no more than textbook knowledge or knowledge researched from internet based sources the night before. Often for some

Know-It-All employees their team is simply a convenient audience or sounding board to offload their knowledge.

Instructions, existing policies and procedures are often seen by them as suggestions inferior to their preferred and superior approach to doing things and therefore will not listen [5] to instructions nor provide plausible alternatives that will get the job done efficiently. Typically, the "superior" ideas they have may not be cost effective, not well thought out, be very time consuming, haphazard, dangerous or even inappropriate for the circumstances, but since they have to have the last word on every subject affecting the team, it becomes a tug of war with the boss. Given that there cannot be two captains on the team; the effect is usually demoralizing [6] to other team members who most likely feel the brunt of the Know-It-All behavior.

The Know-It-All Boss

In the workplace, a boss generally makes decisions in the best interest of his subordinates, nurtures and helps them to reach their potential. Know-It-All bosses on the other hand seem to take to heart the other definition of a boss, that is, "to be master of or over; ... control. ...to order about, esp[ecially] in an arrogant manner. ...to be too domineering and authoritative." [8] As you can imagine, that will be detrimental to the emotional wellbeing of the employees. Know-It-All bosses don't just take to heart the misconstrued definition of a boss, they act it out. Chen and Fast in their Newsweek article about the toxic boss titled "The Making of a Toxic Boss" had this to say: "A recent survey reveals that a startling 37 percent of the country's workforce—some 54 million people—have bosses who scream at them, belittle them, sabotage their work, and are otherwise aggressive." [9] Why will Know-

It-All bosses not belittle subordinates? They believe that subordinates don't know enough or as much as they do or are not as important as they, "the boss." In the rare occasions Know-It-All bosses concede that a subordinate knows enough to be threatening they may resort to sabotaging their work to subjugate them and remind them that the "domain of knowledge" rests with the boss.

Adam Cohen in his Time article titled "New Laws Target Workplace Bullying" brings out the uglier side of Know-It-All bosses. He says: "Bullying bosses scream, often with the goal of humiliating ... Bosses may abuse because they have impossibly high standards, are insecure or have not been properly socialized. But some simply enjoy it." [10] Know-It-All bosses obsessed with perfection will typically set unattainable standards for their subordinates and then resort to the obnoxious behavior of screaming, shouting and sarcastic criticism in other to bully and eventually humiliate their subordinates into emotional wrecks that jump to their every whim. The obsession with perfection and setting unattainable goals probably stems from impractical and unproven knowledge acquired over time, but which Know-It-All bosses feel should be practiced in the workplace setting, at the expense of company resources and time.

Have you ever listened to a Know-It-All boss, who was clueless about your job description or what you actually did for your company, try to finagle or eke out a description to someone? The Know-It-All boss probably never bothered to find out what you did for the company because he already "knew", so why ask you; a subordinate. Have you ever sent an idea to your Know-It-All boss and later you heard the Know-It-All boss presenting it as his idea? But then, if the idea is shut down or dismissed as a bad idea, the Know-It-All boss immediately attributes the idea to you. Of course, "smart" ideas come exclusively from Know-It-All bosses, who also probably think their ideas are "infallible", whereas the bad ideas are something that should come from the subordinates. These circular, self-centered or self gyrating manners of reasoning and behaving are what make Know-It-All bosses difficult to deal with.

The Know-It-All Teacher

Teachers have more knowledge about the subject being thought than their pupils or students. Hence, Know-It-All teachers most often are not exhibiting the Know-It-All behavior based on the domain or subject knowledge they have or are supposed to teach. The problem here ranges from, trying to put down other teachers [11] to showing that other teachers are not as smart as the Know-It-All teacher. Another serious problem is using information or knowledge about a student's private life or weakness [12] in a denigrating manner in front of other students with the end result of thoroughly humiliating the student. [13, 14] Good teachers have professional relationships with their students and in this capacity they learn a lot about the student's private life. Some students unwittingly even entrust their teachers with intimate health and family problems. How could Know-It-All teachers use this acquired intimate knowledge of a student?

Let us answer that question with an example derived from a classroom setting. A Know-It-All teacher learned from a student's parent informally, in confidence, that her daughter Jane was diagnosed with attention deficit hyperactivity disorder and that she was having marital problems with Jane's dad. A few weeks later, Jane answers a question incorrectly and way off point prompting the teacher to comment: "Jane. That comment makes me wonder if you took your ADHD medication this morning. Did you sleep well last night or did your bickering parents keep you up all night?" Clearly, this is the epitome of humiliation in a classroom setting. Some Know-It-All teachers may justify such a disparaging and derogatory comment as stating the "truth" and "helping" Jane explain the reason for her off point comment in class. But the fact is that, such unsolicited, inappropriate disclosure and use of knowledge is unethical and possibly violates various privacy acts. It only serves the hidden agenda of the teacher, that is, to manipulate and control the class students emotionally; even when doing so is damaging to the students emotionally.

Know-It-All teachers have also been known to use class periods to promote their domains of knowledge outside of what they are teaching or outside the curriculum. So then, if the Know-It-All teacher is a fishing aficionado; class projects, class examples, teaching anecdotes and so on, will revolve around fishes and fishing. Such a Know-It-All teacher who teaches history may ask questions like: "What species of fishes are found in Lake Michigan?" or "When in the "history" of Lake Michigan was Brook Trout introduced?" These questions may invariably lead to a long-winded, one-sided lecture on Brook Trout as the Know-It-All teacher propounds his knowledge to the admiration and praise of the class, though the "lecture" is outside the curriculum.

When good teachers are asked a question they cannot answer, normally they will state that they don't know the answer and that they will research and answer during the next class period. Or, they may log onto the internet with the students and quickly locate information that helps answer the question. Not so with Know-It-All teachers. Since they are supposed to know everything, and they lack humility, [15] a typical reaction may be to fabricate something quickly, change the topic and move on. Or, they might resort to berating or condescendingly dismissing the question as irrelevant.

The Know-It-All Student

The Know-It-All student is one of the worst distractions a teacher can have in a classroom. It is almost as if the teacher and the Know-It-All student are competing or jostling for attention in the teacher's class. One Know-It-All behavior exhibited by Know-It-All students is the frequent and incessant corrections [4,16] of the teacher in front of the other students. Not only are they designed to humiliate the teacher most often, but additionally the purpose is to shine and let the class know how smart they are or that they really are "smarter" than the teacher.

Sometimes witty Know-It-All students will frame the correction in the form of a question to mask their intention or true motives. Vainglorious Know-It-All students can also frame mischief in questions drawn from obscure details on the subject being taught, with the true intent being, to humiliate the teacher into admitting that he or she does not know the answer or to trap the teacher in a lie or just to show the other students how smart and how great they are. Most likely the obscure details came from a web search all night long the previous day. In today's teaching environment where students know the curriculum, know what will be taught and what day it will be taught, Know-It-All students could exploit such information for their self serving interest.

Know-It-All students with exaggerated opinion of themselves look and talk down to other students whom they consider inferior, sometimes in a very obnoxious [17] manner. This could be in the form of snide remarks, spreading rumors [18] or a direct affront that sometimes borders on bullying or sometimes directly bullying students they think don't belong to their class of "intelligence" or who are not at par with their level of "brilliance." Computer savvy Know-It-All students could also take the bullying one step further to cyber bullying [19] or e-bullying [20] to maximize the impact and reach a wider audience, with the ultimate desire and purpose of increasing their shine and popularity.

The Know-It-All Boyfriend

Do you have a boyfriend who is constantly correcting your grammar, opinion, personal views, personal taste and other trivial details of your life? Often Know-It-All boyfriends will even tell you how to do your job in your workplace. Furthermore, the corrections invariably lead to heated arguments when your opinion differs somewhat from theirs or your opinion is completely different. The corrections and arguments erupt anywhere and anytime with no regard to who is listening or the appropriateness of the setting. Frequently, the main objective is for them to win the argument and worse still prove you wrong, if not humiliate you for daring to challenge their views or hold your opinion. Forum postings, chat scripts, blogs and the internet in general are replete with literally hundreds of thousands, if not millions, of girlfriends concerned about their Know-It-All boyfriend.

One of the most frequent complaints is the obsession with corrections. [21] While there is nothing wrong with correcting someone from time to time, if done in a respectful, sensitive, caring and appropriate manner, this is not true for Know-It-All boyfriends. Know-It-All boyfriends might see the constant corrections as a way to assert themselves and dominate their girlfriends. Why not? After all, Know-It-All boyfriends have to be "correct" all the time and "win" every argument, since they "know" everything, even if that means alienating their girlfriend. The aforesaid self-centered and self promoting view of Know-It-All boyfriends is the reason it is difficult to have a pleasant conversation with them. The Know-It-All boyfriend's insensitivity and lack of common sense is exemplified in the inability to read his mortified girlfriend's body language [22] when the so-called corrections are made or arguments become very heated.

Positive criticism when provided respectfully and in the proper setting is usually very constructive and upbuilding to the recipient. Know-It-All boyfriends however, seem to wallow in negative criticism, administered relentlessly to ensure their victim is held captive under their vice like control. [23] The negative criticism spans the gamut, from their girlfriend's weight, to how she dresses, the food she cooks, how she talks, how she walks, how she answers the phone and other trivialities of life that can only bother a Know-It-All boyfriend. Of course, if their girlfriend did not "walk" like they think she should "walk" then that is a sign that "they" are loosing "control" over her and other unsubstantiated reasoning that impel Know-It-All boyfriends. Oh yeah, and need we mention, that "walk" that is not the way the Know-It-All boyfriend expects her to "walk," that is because there has to be another boyfriend in the picture! These may sound hilarious, but there are girls and women who have "boyfriends" who are absolutely difficult to reason with because they already know everything and every intention of their girlfriends' heart.

Let us talk about how Know-It-All boyfriends gather the information that eventually makes up part of their knowledge base and which they could use against you in an argument. Have you ever opened your email inbox and saw emails marked as "Read" when you know for certain that you never read them? Then, you remembered that your Know-It-All boyfriend had helped you set up the email account including your login and password. Have you ever spent time wondering why you think your purse was moved from where you left it or that someone has gone through your purse? Or perhaps your cell phone was moved from where you left it? Well, it is probable that your Know-It-All boyfriend was gathering "knowledge" because he has to "know" and make sure everything is under "control." But that is until an argument breaks out and you begin to wonder how he knew you loaned your mother some money. Using personal information, gleaned by observation, stealthily or from conversations, against their loved ones is one of the most annoying threats of a Know-It-All boyfriend. If on the other hand the Know-It-All boyfriend has internet [38] access, at home, on his mobile phone or laptop, then the information gathering especially to win arguments gets notched up to a different level, because now they can argue with "backup," whether the "backup" fits the argument or not.

Sometimes, victims feel as if they live with a Federal agent in the house. This is especially true if every other conversation with the Know-It-All boyfriend is a one-sided domineering and intimidating interrogation. The Know-It-All boyfriend asks the victim: "How was your day at work today?" Then as the victim answers, an argument erupts as he gets preoccupied with the negative trivia and minutia of the victim's response. While narrating what happened at work, a statement like: "... my boss came over..." gets knee-jacked out of proportion and construed with all sorts of insulting and condescending innuendos on the part of the Know-It-All boyfriend with the sole intent to humiliate, possibly manipulate and have the victim under his control.

The Know-It-All Girlfriend

Know-It-All girlfriends share practically the same Know-It-All behavior as the Know-It-All boyfriend described in the section above, especially the incessant public and private corrections [24, 25] as well as the negative sarcastic criticism; hence, we will not repeat those same Know-It-All manifestations in this section. However, have you ever had a Know-It-All girlfriend who was always second guessing everything you said? Somehow, saying you just stopped by on your way back from work was not enough, she had to smell [26] your clothes, to make sure there is no strange perfume emanating. She walks you back to your car, she spends a few minutes inspecting the car to make sure the seat position has not changed and there are no foreign hairs or articles "she" did not leave behind. The Know-It-All girlfriend has to gather all that "knowledge" to be sure everything is under "control." What prompts the Know-It-All girlfriend to behave this way? Of course, she already "knows" you are cheating; she just needs to show you how "smart" she is by proving it. How does she "know" you are cheating? Female intuition is the first answer Know-It-All girlfriends will throw out to justify their inappropriate behavior and presumption. Female intuition is not being castigated here, since sometimes that intuition is dead correct, but then, in those instances women had justifiable rational to suspect something and they don't go about smelling or searching a boyfriend routinely or constantly or capriciously.

Have you ever gone shopping with a Know-It-All girlfriend and she insists, without your consent or consulting you first, to choose your outfits for you? Or perhaps she drops by your place with her girlfriends and she spends time showing your place to her girlfriends, and that is fine, but then she is pointing out things that need to be fixed, tossed out, gross, not acceptable, replaced and so on; without consulting you first? Of course, as a Know-It-All girlfriend, why consult with you the boyfriend, she already "knows" the best outfit for you and "knows" precisely how your place should look like! Such disrespectful and condescending or supercilious attitudes most often is the Know-It-All girlfriend's way of showing they know everything.

The Know-It-All Husband

Know-It-All husbands display the same Know-It-All behavior of incessant humiliating corrections as well as the negative sarcastic criticism described in the Know-It-All boyfriend section above. The Know-It-All husband's constant faultfinding and obsession with correctitude, perhaps out of a sense of superiority, or perhaps as a husband who "knows" everything, often wittingly or unwittingly makes his wife feel stupid [27] and unloved. One would think that the discomfort their wives felt when they behave this way would make Know-It-All husbands to rethink their behavior, but that is usually not the case. Most often the corrections are for trivial [28] things that can be lovingly overlooked. Perhaps for such Know-It-All husbands overlooking such trivial corrections will be foregoing an important control tool. Obviously, few Know-It-All husbands would have the nerve to correct their boss at work or their parents or some important personality they admired, since that will be disrespectful. However, as soon as they get home to their wives the respectful approach to talking gets tossed to the winds.

The unexplainable need to be an unsolicited spokesperson [29] for their wives is another issue that puts Know-It-All husbands on collision course with their wives. In these scenarios, when a question is posed to a wife and before she can respond or in mid sentence, the Know-It-All husband takes over and answers. Of course, he can "read" his wife's mind, so that is why he cuts her off and asserts his dominion before onlookers. This uncouth overbearing behavior as a mouthpiece for the wife may stem from numerous wife "correcting" sessions, to the point that the Know-It-All husband actually begins to think it is better he answers the questions posed since he is the "smarter" mate. Or perhaps it stems from the need to retain the center of attention and shine, on his "brilliant" self as the Know-It-All husband.

Another annoying habit of Know-It-All husbands is, condescendingly explaining useless and trivial details to their wives as if they were talking to a second grader. Yes, some will actually do that in public, specifically to show how "detailed" they are, while humiliating their wives and portraying their wives as incompetent. Now, let us touch the famous "men never listen" while you are talking to them. This certainly applies to Know-It-All husbands. But why should they listen to their wives or anybody for that matter? They already "know" what you want to say before you say it! This ill Know-It-All behavior most likely arises from not being open to alternative opinions or sound reasoning, as well as the possibility that the Know-It-All husband is spinning mental cycles preparing for a counter response or attack, even when he has not heard a word that was spoken to him.

The Know-It-All Wife

Know-It-All wives display the same Know-It-All behavior of incessant humiliating corrections [24, 30] as well as the negative sarcastic criticism [23] described in the Know-It-All husband section above. It is normal in a loving relationship to ask for explanations about things we don't understand or perhaps things that confuse us or make us uncomfortable. It is certainly loving for a husband and wife to participate in the decision making process of the couple. However, Know-It-All wives take this one step farther by constantly challenging and relentlessly demanding explanation for every trivial detail, decision, comment and so on, literally arguing [31] their husband into the ground. This is probably to show how "smart" they are or how much they "know" about everything or how keen they are to "know" every single detail possible about the unknown or to remind there husbands that they are not to be trifled with or a burning need to be "right" all the time.

It is certainly loving, and expected, for a wife to remind the husband about important things from time to time. However, when a Know-It-All wife, who "knows" all the important "details" of the family, takes it upon herself to call incessantly to remind her husband, at work for example, of trivial stuff that can wait until he gets home, this might come across as lack of confidence in his abilities to remember such trivialities or perhaps that he is so forgetful and "dumb" that he needs to be reminded constantly of trivialities like a two year old child.

Other condescending preoccupations with trivialities include Know-It-All wives putting sticky notes all over the house to remind their husbands about trivial things as if they were mentally impaired. "Brush or wipe your feet before entering the house." "No shoes in the kitchen." "Flush the toilet after use." "Turn the bedroom lights off after use." "Place used dishes in the sink." "Leave the toilet flap down." "Don't sit butt naked on the sofa." "No smelly socks in the living room." And the list goes on. Clearly, all the aforesaid are important reminders and are needed for the smooth functioning of the house. But, what ever happened to respectfully and gently communicating these reminders by conversation to a husband, especially at appropriate and opportune moments, repeatedly if necessary, but not when he is hurrying to catch the train or an NFL game? Of course, a Know-It-All wife already "knows" these things and just needs to "educate" the husband, even when that comes across as humiliating. Just think for a moment, if the husband's friends come over and somehow run into some of those sticky notes that were not removed, how humiliating can that be!

Then, there is the Know-It-All wives behavior of giving useless hints and cues in public; while their husbands are talking, as if to help their "dumb" husband remember trivial details in a conversation. At least, that is what an observer watching the cues and hints will conclude. Sometimes, this takes the form of incessantly interrupting the husband's comment or narrative to interject a missing trivial detail, as if the listeners knew there were missing details. Of course, as the "smarter" of the pair, Know-It-All wives take it upon themselves to keep interjecting that way to make sure the husband is saying the "right" thing always, even when this behavior makes the husband very uncomfortable visibly.

Know-It-All wives sometimes have this large mental "database" of men and what they do, have done and will do. So then, unceasingly they retrieve personality traits and profiles from this database to vocally dress down their husband and compare them. This tendency to show how much they "know" about men drives a wedge into the daily conversation with their husbands who is constantly on the defensive against the selected profile from the "database" and the humiliating implications of such a comparison.

The Know-It-All Friend

A good friend normally is there "for" us. Some Know-It-All friends are usually there "with" us suffocating us with their incessant meddling and desire to "know" everything we are doing and to make sure "they" approve what we are doing or that it meets there "approval!" "Oh, so you bought a new wrist watch. Why did you not tell me you were going to buy one?" In other words, you did not receive their approval to buy one or what? The Know-It-All behavior of incessant humiliating corrections [32, 33] as well as the negative sarcastic criticism [34] described earlier is common place behavior for Know-It-All friends.

Obsessed with the fervent desire to be "right" always, Know-It-All friends will dominate conversations to the discomfort of their friends and discard opposing or contrary opinions with flourish. Then, there is the constant countering of arguments, such that it does not matter what the point of view or comment or opinion their friends hold, Know-It-All friends who counter point of views will often have the exact opposite and "correct" opinion. "That mall is not so bad," comments their friend. "No, the mall is so-so," a Know-It-All friend quips back. Of course, theirs is always the "correct" opinion because they "know" everything including synonyms! No wonder, sometimes, friends see Know-It-All friends like enemies.

For some Know-It-All friends, you have to live up to and meet their "standards" of what a "good" friend should be. They already "know" these standards, it is up to "you" as their "privileged" friend to learn and live up to them. Sometimes these standards may include obsession with and expectations of perfection in words, thoughts and deeds from you their friend, so "you" can continue to "qualify" to be called their friend on their terms, perhaps because they already "know" what is good for the friendship.

For some Know-It-All friends with an exaggerated and pompous opinion of themselves, your friendship with them is not a friendship of equals, of course, they are doing you a favor and it is a "privilege" to be called their friend. This incorrect view of friendship is demonstrated in the condescending and patronizing way some Know-It-All friends talk to their friends. Or, even in the manner in which they give advice to their friends, "as if they were talking to a child." [39] "Ok Stephanie, here is rule number one if you want us to remain friends. When I walk past the Grocery Manager without saying hello, I expect you as friend to do the same. That is what I expect from my friends." As if Stephanie shares the same uppity views with her Know-It-All friend.

Another irritating quirk of Know-It-All friends is the ardent desire to be the center of attention and the "shine." So much so that anywhere you go with them they have to be the ones shinning or else they will not rest easy. Once the attention is on you and not your Know-It-All friend, some Know-It-All friends have been known to fake injury, sickness, throw tantrums, negatively criticize the event and everything associated with it, want to leave the event or decide to do other weird things designed to take the shine away from "you" and return it on "them." Of course, of what good was the event; if everybody was not admiring and praising your Know-It-All friend?

How about Know-It-All friends with no common sense? They arrive at the gasoline station with you and then suddenly change their mind and drive off. They "know" that the price is five cents cheaper at another gas station they saw on the "internet" and so they drive five miles to the other gas station and drive five miles back to save a buck on the cost of filling their gasoline tank. What of the "real" cost of driving ten miles including wear and tear? As if the "internet" is the panacea for common sense. What can be said about Know-It-All friends who spend all their annual vacation time in the first six weeks of the year! Why? Oh, because they were going to buy more vacation time from their employer anyway. Of course, they can buy vacation time with air and not money. It is their money they remind you quickly, so don't try reasoning or crunching numbers, because they already "know" the cost. Then there are the Know-It-All friends who call you to borrow rent money; they are one month behind, they tell you. About a month later, you get another call, now they are two months behind. How is that possible? You did lend them money for the month in arrears. Oh, they had to pay for their fitness club overdue dues and secure a layaway in a retail store they were about to lose. Of course, they "know" those were more important than paying their rent; the reason for which they borrowed the money. Don't try reasoning with them because you may be reminded that they "know" everything including how to manage their priorities.

Have you ever sneezed, washed your hand with soap and water and a Know-It-All friend still handed you a hand sanitizer in front of everybody, explaining to them the details of another non-contagious ailment you have that has nothing to do with sneezing? Of course, such Know-It-All friends "know" you did not wash your hands "correctly" and they are only watching out for your health. Have you ever had a nosy Know-It-All friend answer your phone, unsolicited, while you are standing right there? He or she had to "know" or acquire "information" right? Even when you let it slide, they don't seem to read your facial expression or body language that shows your displeasure of the intrusion; and some Know-It-All friends will do it again. Have you ever invited a Know-It-All friend to your house and, without asking, he or she begins a grand bedroom to bedroom tour of the house on this first visit, unaccompanied? Sometimes the tour ends at your refrigerator, where he or she partakes liberally of your food and goodies. Why not? That is why you are a "friend" and they already "know" you will not mind. Such faulty reasoning is probably the reason proffered by Know-It-All friends for taking advantage of your hospitality and showing little or no respect for your privacy and the honor of asking first.

The Know-It-All Neighbor

We all have good neighbors who are very helpful, very friendly and lookout for our well being. We also enjoy having conversations with them. However, is it not also true that there is always that one in-your-face Know-It-All Neighbor or the covert or sly Know-It-All Neighbor who leaves us with a lot of trepidation and anxiety when they suddenly "appear" from nowhere, uninvited and at the most inopportune moment. Possibly driven by the desire to "know" what you are up to, what that noise is about, what you are cooking that smells so good, why you are remodeling, why you are all dressed up and so forth. Those are not bad to ask or to know from your neighbor, but it is the Know-It-All Neighbor's incessant intrusion that is a problem. They have to know everything, perhaps, to provide them with gossip fodder to share with the other neighbors.

The constant intrusion of the Know-It-All Neighbor becomes even more annoying when they always have to "teach" you something you are not doing "right" in your daily chores. Some Know-It-All Neighbors will even give you their used tool that is supposed to be "superior" to the brand new one, of a different make than theirs, you just bought. Even more irritating is the fact that they know you just bought the tool. The giving, although appreciated, was more for self aggrandizement. Well, how about Know-It-All Neighbors who will offer and insist on helping out in intimate personal chores when they come over?

Some in-your-face Know-It-All Neighbors will deliberately buy things, say things or do things to foment competition that will show how smart, how fast and how quick they are. It is almost as if you are constantly pitting wits with them. You buy a 1.2-liter engine lawn mower, they buy a 1.5-liter engine lawn mower and talk nonstop about how theirs is greater, the state of the art and so on. Then there are the hostile and confrontational Know-It-All Neighbors who will counter and argue you down about almost anything to prove they are smarter or more experienced than you, especially when you disagree with there self serving opinions. "I mow my lawn in a circle for fun," you say in a relaxed tête-à-tête with them across the fence and they respond "No, you should mow it diagonally, that is the "recommended" way of mowing lawns "correctly"." As if there is a Federal Regulation on lawn mowing!

Furthermore, there are the Know-It-All Neighbors who are rarely original in their suggestions or advice, always feeding off the creative expressions of others in the neighborhood and then make other people's ideas appear like coming from their great and brilliant self. Meanwhile, you could literally turn around and see that all your neighbors have done what is being proffered as an ingenious and novel idea. Moreover, remember the "vigilante" Know-It-All Neighbor, the one who seems to peek through his or her window blind at the most inopportune moments. When you crank your car up very early in the morning, when you return very late at night, when you are scantily clad and relaxing in your backyard or poolside, on Saturday mornings when you run to the mailbox a bit frumpily dressed; they have their "eyes" on you, because they need to "know" that you are "safe." We all appreciate watchful neighbors, but when "vigilante" Know-It-All Neighbors monitor your every single move on your property it can be very disconcerting, annoying and emotionally draining.

The Know-It-All Stranger

We meet strangers everywhere and generally in public places. They are very helpful with the information they provide for us, in fact sometimes their tips and words of caution have saved lives or made a difference in our lives, one way or another. Normally, when we meet people for the first time in a public place we have civil conversations about whatever subject and divulge as little personal information as is safely possible. However, some Know-It-All strangers seem to take it upon themselves to really get "know" everything during that first short encounter, asking penetrating personal and private questions that make you squirm and feel like you have been backed into a wall. Then, with each answer you give they "drill" deeper and counter your attempts to change the conversation. Since Know-It-All strangers want to "acquire" as much information as possible they fail to observe the consternation on your face and your body language showing how appalled you are at their audacity. Here is the part that "kills" us or lives us astonished; they get off at the next bus stop or their flight is announced next and they walk away! What was all that arm-twisting interrogation and cross-examination about?

Grilling others with inappropriate questions is not the only faux pas of Know-It-All strangers, they could dominate conversations on any subject raised, insolently cutting off every other persons' contributions. Of course, Know-It-All strangers do this to ensure that their "brilliance" is untainted and so we can leave the scene enthralled and wondering who that "brilliant" stranger was, and oh yes, wishing we will meet them again so they can treat us like trash! Then, there are the Know-It-All strangers who are generally loud and exhibitionistic in all its ramifications. They are seated five rows ahead of you on a flight to Macau, but you can hear them blab intimate family information, disseminate other information that makes them sound important or that is phrased to elevate them above everyone else within earshot. Talking about the housing market with brilliant statistics is a precursor to how great and how expensive their newly acquired home is. And, oh yes, they "cheated" the whole worldwide housing market and bought there house for the bargain price of one and a half million dollars! Talking about the tight job market invariably leads to telling total strangers how they got a new job in a prestigious company as the vice president of some fancy department and a seven digit paycheck with impeccable pecks!

Some Know-It-All strangers will quickly zero in on another stranger who is sharing the shine in a public conversation and attack them verbally with hostile questions aimed at taking an edge off their shine and ensuring the shine is reverted to only them as the most "brilliant" or as the "funniest" stranger in the vicinity. Other Know-It-All strangers will have no qualms zeroing in on the most taciturn in the conversation group and humiliating them with pointed personal questions aimed at making the Know-It-All stranger look "funny" and "great."

The Know-It-All Mother

Our mothers are older than we are and definitely have had more experience in life than we have. Additionally, a good mother's counsel and advice, even when it does not come across suavely, are for our good and well being. The problem however arises when Know-It-All mothers create the impression that they are above reproach or misspeaking or making judgment errors. [34] Even when all evidence indicates they do, like we all do. But then, if Know-It-All mothers admitted to misspeaking or judgment errors that would mean they did not "know" everything. This leads to a vicious cycle of perhaps telling more lies to defend older lies, as the Know-It-All mother tries to prove everybody wrong and prove she is right, and the endless argument continues. Sometimes the only way to end such arguments especially with her children is the famous: "Do as I say because I'm your mother."

Does your Know-It-All mother sneak up behind you or eavesdrop or pickup the phone extension while you are on the phone? Naturally, they want to "know" who you are talking with on the phone and what you are talking about. Although there is an appropriate way to find out who their child is talking to on the phone and what they are talking about, Know-It-All mothers probably prefer to catch their children "red-handed" in the act, even when this will alienate them and make them look very distrustful. How about Know-It-All mothers sneaking into a child's room while their child is in the shower, for example, to check their cell phones? Whatever happened to telling your child face to face, that you will, from time to time, check his or her cell phone for sexting, obscene messages and other inappropriate uses of his or her cell phone? That face to face conversation by itself is a form of deterrent. Probably, the need to "know" everything and every detail overrides the decency and respect due to children.

Most mothers usually spend some time and get to know the friends of their children and then counsel their children appropriately against bad influence. Not so for a Know-It-All mother, she already "knows" her child's friend is bad because he lives in the rough part of town. "Everyone" who lives in the rough part of town is bad. The Know-It-All mother may even go a step further than these presumptions and try to sabotage the friendship with ludicrous telephone gimmicks like: "Oh, he is not here" when the child is standing right there and listening to the lie with consternation or "He is asleep" when he is watching television or "We are eating right now" when he is outside playing.

The mother-in-law [36] and daughter-in-law rivalry is hard to decipher. But sometimes if the mother-in-law is a Know-It-All mother, then, most likely because she "knows" everything she is in her daughter-in-law's apartment or house trying to "teach" her how things should be done, that is, the "correct" way of doing things. As if the "correct" way of boiling water is worth the peace and the cordial relationship a good mother-in-law should enjoy with her daughter-in-law.

Another Know-It-All mother issue is verbally telling a child they will be up to no good and persistently drumming that into the child's head daily. Of course, the Know-It-All mother can "read" the future, so they already "know" [34] how the child's future will turn out. Some Know-It-All mothers even many years into their child's successful adulthood, still retain the grudge and erroneous prediction. Why not? If they retracted that statement, it will indicate they don't "know" everything, so they hold onto the disproved opinion. Incessant corrections, nit picking and negative sarcastic criticism of their children, by Know-It-All mothers can also have a debilitating [35] effect on children.

The Know-It-All Father

Just like mothers, our fathers have more experience than we have in life. Their counsel and guidance help us to get the first male perspective of the world, that is, the world as seen by men. We may not always have agreed with their views or their perspective, but one thing is certain, and that is; good fathers have the good intentions on their children at heart always. Know-It-All fathers however share some of the Know-It-All behavior described above for Know-It-All mothers including the incessant humiliating corrections as well as the negative sarcastic criticism directed toward their children and wife.

Know-It-All fathers sometimes take the well worn cliché "Father knows best" too literal. This is usually evident when their children, grownups or teenagers or preteens, approach them with a problem or a question, for which they are completely clueless. Of course, as a father who "knows" everything or who thinks he is supposed to know everything, or as the family "encyclopedia", the instinctive reaction is to fabricate, and in doing so, maintain the Know-It-All status quo. Sometimes, when they observe their children trying to resolve lives problems on their own, with some measure of success, they will interfere and insist on their resolution as superior, even when it is just another alternative or sometimes an inaccurate solution. Whatever happened to admitting that they don't know the answer and then researching it together with their child, perhaps as a family project? Or simply saying that the data requested does not exist currently in their mental "encyclopedia" but will be updated shortly from data sources.

One of the most frequently heard complaints leveled against men in general, including husband and fathers is that they will not stop to ask for driving directions, especially when they have no GPS navigation system on board or mounted in their vehicle. Let us look at it from a Know-It-All father's point of view. He has spent the last twenty minutes looking for a specific street; his teenage son is already ten minutes late to an event and he keeps ignoring his son's request that they ask someone at the myriads of gas stations they drove by. Think about it for a second, why should the Know-It-All father ask anyone? He already "knows" the whole city by heart! That is the reason he has no maps and no GPS navigation system, additionally, stopping to ask will belittle him and show he does not know everything. This refusal to ask for directions is an indirect way of rejecting other people's inputs or points of views or opinion, a typical Know-It-All behavior. This could also be related to the reason why men are not too worried about their health. "According to a 2001 CDC report, women are 33% more likely than men to visit a doctor in general" [37] even though "men die at higher rates than women from the top 10 causes of death." Why should Know-It-All fathers visit a doctor? They already "know" they are alright and some may even vocalize that response, even when their wives and children are insisting they don't look alright and require a doctor's immediate attention.

Some Know-It-All fathers also dominate conversations in the family with long-winded, one-sided lectures, with family members barely able to squeeze in a word or two. The Know-It-All father in this scenario asks a question and does not allow an answer or a comment. "Who took the ten dollar bill from the table in my bedroom?" Before anyone answers, "John, you took the money because I saw you enter my bedroom." As if the other children never entered the bedroom also. But then, he is a Know-It-All father so he already "knows" who took the money without waiting for the answer before accusing.

The Know-It-All Child

A good son or daughter brings joy to the heart of their parents, especially as the parents see their child blossom into a responsible caring adult. In fact, some of the closest relationships that exist are between mothers and daughters or between fathers and sons or combinations thereof. The Know-It-All behavior in a child starts at a stage [40] in their life, typically in the early preteens. A common complaint is talking back [40] to the parents, or questioning instructions to them on how to perform a task, not because the Know-It-All child did not understand the instruction but perhaps, because they "know" another way of accomplishing the task, even when this is based on an exaggerated opinion of their ability. Invariably, firmly saying "No" to the Know-It-All child leads to them being more assertive [41] about their opinion which in turn spirals into an annoying and obnoxious [41] argument.

Know-It-All children can also dominate [41] conversations just like adults, to the point that even adults cannot chip in a word edgewise. Sometimes this domination is transferred to interactions with siblings. No only will they not listen to their sibling's views and opinions but ensure that their opinions and views are predominantly echoed over and over again to the annoyance or anger of their siblings. The dominion of the domination can also extend to where they are intrusively telling parents and siblings what to do. But then, how can a Know-It-All child listen to their siblings? They already "know" what their siblings have in mind, so why let them voice it out? Besides, that would be like the siblings telling them what they already know. Sometimes such erroneous reasoning leads to sibling rivalry and fights.

Do you have a Know-It-All child who is always correcting [42] you or correcting everybody around them? [43] This is another complaint against Know-It-All children. It is almost as if the parents are competing with the Know-It-All child. This incessant correction can be very irritating if not downright annoying, since often the corrections are trivial and miniscule nuances in expressions. "The sky is blue today," says the parent smiling at her child, who quickly counters, "No mummy! The sky is light blue today." Of course, the five year old "knows" more grammar than the mother who thought her all she knows up till that point.

The double life Know-It-All child is difficult to comprehend. The double life, with the double cell phones, double clothes, double makeup styles, double shoes, double school bags, pretending to be an obedient and cooperative child at home, but disobeying parental guidance outside the home, indicates that Know-It-All children are aware of what parents expect of them, but they choose to do the opposite outside the home. Of course, they "know" better than their parents, so outside the home they "live" out what is forbidden by their parents. That is until their bad conduct comes to light, bringing shame and heart ache to parents and them alike.

Know-It-All children sometimes carry their behavior to school and foment trouble in school which includes challenging teachers disrespectfully, bullying, e-bullying, e-harassing and so on, to the point that parents are constantly called to their Know-It-All child's school to receive complaints.

The Know-It-All Brother or Sister

Know-It-All brothers or sisters sometimes call you out of the blues to tell you what you need to do right then, about something going on in your life for which they are "really" clueless. They heard something from somebody who lives somewhere and decided to call you, because they "know" what "you" had to do to "fix" your problem. Or may be they call you and request money for a product they "ordered" for you because they "know" you will like it. Whatever happened to asking questions first before acting as an unsolicited adviser or product merchant for a sibling?

As we discussed earlier in the Know-It-All child section, sibling domination of conversations, the relentless correction [44] of siblings and sibling rivalry [45] are sometimes carried into the adult life of brothers and sisters. As can be expected, sibling rivalry is even more toxic when a Know-It-All brother or sister craves to be the center of attention and to shine in various family settings, even as adults. Sometimes the only credentials for being the center of attention are because they are the oldest, or the only sibling who finished a two-year college, or the only sibling who attempted Law School and dropped out, or even better, the first sibling to have visited New York, or the only sibling who has flown in an airplane, or the only sibling with a house, or the only sibling with an expensive car and other inane credentials; as if an outsider looking in knows or cares about any of those concocted credentials.

How about Know-It-All brothers or sisters who are frustratingly demanding? Behaving like you owe them money or behaving like they are orphaned and you suddenly became their parents. "I know you have the money," they will glibly tell you, when you voice your exasperation. Of course, they "know" you have the money, because your bank sends copies of your bank statement to them for approval first, as a needy sibling, after which the bank forwards them to you. Then there are the Know-It-All brothers or sisters who are prone to lies. They will fabricate stories nonstop to extract money from you. None of the stories ever check out and usually there are more stories to "backup" old stories that never panned out. Ah, yes, they always contact you because they "know" you are the only one who can buy into their self-centered, self absorbed and manipulative yarns.

The Know-It-All Forum or Chat Room Geek

Forum, weblog or blog, message board, chat room, etc. geeks are usually technologically savvy and or know very profoundly the domain or body of knowledge being discussed or posted. They are also adept at using hints, cues and explanatory responses in a very respectful and dignifying manner to get everyone up to speed on the subject at hand. They offer help sincerely when requested without wresting the dignity of the requester.

However, have you ever been in a chat room or even a forum posting and this particular Know-It-All forum or chat room geek had an opposite and negative response or answer to almost everything you ever said or typed? It was as if the Know-It-All forum or chat room geek only saw your response, in fact, it felt as if this person could smell each time your finger touched your keyboard, because this Know-It-All forum or chat room geek fired a salvo back to the screen almost immediately. Then, in the heat of the exchange, you begin to omit words or commit grammatical errors in your sentences and the Know-It-All forum or chat room geek zeros in on those errors and humiliates you even further, making your day miserable.

Know-It-All forum or chat room geeks sometimes are obsessed with correcting [44] other peoples grammatical errors even in such an informal setting as a chat room where members are typing away furiously with abandon, at the pace or intensity of the conversation at hand. Could such preoccupation with grammatical content in the heat of a conversation be indicative of a Know-It-All forum or chat room geek who really does not have much to say [44] or contribute? Could a focused destructive criticism of what other members are creatively contributing to the conversation indicate lack of originality on the part of the Know-It-All forum or chat room geek? The inclination is to answer in the affirmative to both questions. Additionally, the correction is sometimes done in such a condescending manner that humiliates the corrected person. It is important to differentiate between correcting a native speaker of a language and someone who is learning the language. Part of learning a new language is being humbly open to corrections almost like a child. However, for native speakers who have a grasp of the language corrections are perceived differently.

The scenario mentioned earlier, where a Know-It-All forum or chat room geek zeros in on one member can also further deteriorate into e-bullying and e-harassing as their comments becomes "obscene and insulting." [46] E-bullying which accounts for about one third [46] of bullying is pervasive in many online activities where people meet and interact virtually.

For unscrupulous Know-It-All forum or chat room geeks the perceived anonymity of forums blogs, message boards, chat rooms, etc. engenders the exaggeration of trivial facts and statistics or outright lies, counting on the fact that, may be, nobody will bother to verify their exaggerated responses or lies. Meanwhile in the heat of conversation, the exaggerated response or lie is self serving; to promote the Know-It-All forum or chat room geek as being "smart" and "great" to other members.

The Know-It-All Social Networker

Various social networks facilitate forums, weblogs or blogs, message boards, chat rooms, etc for members. Hence, some Know-It-All social networkers behave like the Know-It-All forum or chat room geek described above. Additionally, since members of some social networks can create profiles, Know-It-All social networkers intent on using their technological savvy or know-how to hurt, humiliate and denigrate others will create fake [47, 48] profile pages that impersonate other members. In these fake profile pages Know-It-All social networkers or "keyboard warriors" [46] will include disparaging remarks, mischievous comments and content that thoroughly damages the character of their target victim.

As we have seen in this chapter, Know-It-Alls can hurt us with the knowledge they possess at least in two ways; by the way they "use" knowledge about us and around us and the way they "acquire" knowledge about us and around us. Knowledge about us, as was described earlier, include intimate entrusted private information, our flaws, weaknesses, etc., while the knowledge around us, constitute the publicly available knowledge about any subject in which we have interest in discussing with the Know-It-All. Clearly, there are more types of Know-It-Alls, but the ones profiled above give us a good picture of how Know-It-Alls use knowledge to hurt others and the different manifestations of their behavior.

Now, let us answer some of the questions posed in chapter 1 which include: Of all the people we associate with on a daily basis who is most likely to be an agonizing Know-It-All? Who is more likely to be a Know-It-All between your best friend or your father, between you and your boyfriend or girlfriend, between you and your husband or wife, between a teacher and a student, between a mother and a father, between you and your brother or sister, between a friend and a stranger, between your boss and your husband or wife, between your boss and your co-worker?

Note that Table 3 below answers these questions based on the relative amount of pages, thoughts, comments, complaints, blogs, postings and so on that were agglomerated from the page count result. While relatively speaking there is no difference in the top five items, it is however surprising to see that children are more likely to display the Know-It-All behavior than either parent and that students are more likely to display the Know-It-All behavior than teachers who teach them. The top five items also suggest that we are likely to experience the Know-It-All behavior from someone very close to us or someone we live with or someone we love dearly than from a stranger or from our boss at work, and this probably explains why there are so many complaints. These people feel the pinch and pressure of the Know-It-All behavior on a daily basis.

Table 3 - Table of Keywords of Some Types of Know-It-All

#	Keywords Searched	Result	#	Keywords Searched	Result
1	"Know-It-All" AND Friend	23.4 million	10	"Know-It-All" AND Student	3.99 million
2	"Know-It-All" AND Wife	23.3 million	11	"Know-It-All" AND Sister	3.58 million
3	"Know-It-All" AND Girlfriend	23.2 million	12	"Know-It-All" AND Teacher	3.48 million
4	"Know-It-All" AND Husband	23.1 million	13	"Know-It-All" AND Boss	2.65 million
5	"Know-It-All" AND Boyfriend	22.9 million	14	"Know-It-All" AND Stranger	2.30 million
6	"Know-It-All" AND Child	5.83 million	15	"Know-It-All" AND Neighbor	2.16 million

7	"Know-It-All" AND Mother	5.37 million	16	"Know-It-All" AND Employee	1.61 million
8	"Know-It-All" AND Brother	5.12 million	17	"Know-It-All" AND Co-worker	0.94 million
9	"Know-It-All" AND Father	4.66 million			

Source: Google.com search results - 01/07/2011

So, are men more likely than women to be Know-It-Alls? If you examine items 2 to 5 as well as other gender based keywords in Table 3 above and group the numbers by gender, it does not provide a clear picture. To break the tie, other search engines were consulted and the more complex Table 4 below answers the question very clearly. There were more than twice as much complaints and writings and thoughts relating to the female gender and than the male gender, meaning that women are more likely to be Know-It-Alls than men. Additionally, if we take Table 5 in chapter 6 into consideration and the fact that the most complained about Know-It-All behavior is the unrelenting and condescending barrage of corrections, then we can presumptively conclude that women are more likely to exhibit this specific Know-It-All behavior than men. Remember that these are simply order of magnitude estimates and common sense, they were not statistically derived. Furthermore, other reasons may account for the differences.

Table 4 - Table of Keywords of Some Types of Know-It-All

#	Keywords Searched	Average	Google	Bing	Yahoo
2	"Know-It-All" AND Wife	68.1 million	23.3 million	90.7 million	90.2 million
3	"Know-It-All" AND Girlfriend	13.9 million	23.2 million	8.98 million	9.47 million
7	"Know-It-All" AND Mother	78.1 million	5.37 million	118 million	111 million
11	"Know-It-All" AND Sister	16.5 million	3.58 million	23.9 million	22.0 million
	Total For Women	**176.6 million**			
4	"Know-It-All" AND Husband	18.7 million	23.1 million	16.5 million	16.4 million
5	"Know-It-All" AND Boyfriend	9.10 million	22.9 million	2.13 million	2.13 million
8	"Know-It-All" AND Brother	22.0 million	5.12 million	30.9 million	30.1 million
9	"Know-It-All" AND Father	26.8 million	4.66 million	39.6 million	36.2 million
	Total For Men	**76.6 million**			

Source: Google.com search results, Bing.com search results and Yahoo.com - 01/07/2011

Much later we will distill out all the Know-It-All manifestations described in this chapter and discuss them in more detail, but first, let us look at the Know-It-All's domain of knowledge. In the next chapter we will talk briefly about the different domains or bodies of knowledge where Know-It-Alls seem to focus their energy or specialize in when displaying the Know-It-All behavior.

Chapter 5: The Know-It-Alls' Domain or Body of Knowledge

As humans we excel in certain aspects of life. Know-It-Alls generally exhibit their behavior in certain domains or bodies of knowledge. Or we could say they have areas of specialty and if you venture into that area of specialty in a conversation with them, you may not leave unscathed. Basically, don't get a Know-It-All started in their domain of expertise. We will look at some of these domains of expertise in this chapter. The bodies of knowledge described in this chapter are by no means exhaustive and some have been aggregated for simplicity. Furthermore, some Know-It-Alls are capable of exhibiting the Know-It-All behavior, when engaged in conversations, across many of these domains.

Grammar

While it is difficult to measure a Know-It-All's knowledge of a language's morphology and syntax, it is clear that some of these Know-It-Alls, whose area of specialization is correcting other people's grammar, are themselves not grammatically competent in the language they are correcting. This is because often when the so-called corrections are reviewed, albeit informally, by a true grammar expert, they fall short. At other times the corrections are truly trivial and simply condescending. For example, someone says: "That is a burgundy colored truck." A Know-It-All responds: "No, that is a darkish purple colored truck." These types of grammatical correction call into question the Know-It-All's grammatical prowess. Although grammatical correction is a way to help us learn and improve our grammar, there is a place and time for everything. There is an appropriate way to correct people, furthermore trivial and inappropriate corrections are best left out of everyday conversations. However, whether a Know-It-Alls' grammatical corrections are made out of a burning need to demonstrate their superiority over another person or the impulsive obsession to correct others, the incessant grammatical correction humiliates and causes anxiety for their victims. Seriously!

Manners

Know-It-Alls who are manner specialists pride themselves in knowing what is customarily acceptable and what is inappropriate, most often based on the culture, environment and background where they grew up. Since they "know" everything about manners, it does not occur to them that some manners are applicable locally, while some are global, besides the person displaying the lack of manners may be visiting. So for example, if it is customary in the culture were a Know-It-All was raised not to give or receive things with the left hand, a Know-It-All may assume this applies in all cultures and launch into a condescending and sometimes denigrating verbal expletive when someone uses their left hand to give or take something. There are numerous culturally isolated or related manners and hence it is unfair to expect someone visiting or not familiar with those manners to conform to them. Even when globally accepted manners like showing respect for the elderly or giving up our seat to an elderly person are not followed by someone, there is no reason for Know-It-Alls to capitalize on such a flaw there and then to fire off a few "knowledge bullets" about manners and what the victim should have done or said, to the humiliation and embarrassment of the victim.

Opinion

Some Know-It-Alls specialize in attacking, rejecting and countering other peoples opinions regardless of its merit, especially if doing so will further their own opinions. This behavior would seem to be worse if there is a sizeable audience before whom the opinions are being presented. Another propelling factor is the need to shine or show how great Know-It-Alls are at debating, even when their opinions lack solid argument or any pragmatic value. However, since it is just an opinion or the Know-It-All's point of view, their victims frequently don't mind respecting the Know-It-All's opinion. The reverse is never true and that is what leads to the standoff as the Know-It-All is bent on vanquishing or subjugating the victim's opinion and or discarding it as incorrect or inferior. For example, a victim may say: "It is a nice day today, it is warm and the sun is shining." A Know-It-All may counter with: "No, it is not a good day, it is windy and allergy sufferers don't find that funny." Or "No, it is not a good day; it is going to rain heavily later tonight." Invariably a prolonged argument may ensue as the Know-It-All battles with a sheath full of words, mostly synonyms, to prove they are "right" or to have the last word.

Weight

Have you ever met someone who seems to always tell you that you lost or gained weight? It is almost as if these Know-It-Alls who specialize in talking about other people's weight have weight scales in their eyes used to scan people and then "know" right there and then that the person they scanned gained or lost weight before asking the person. Then, there are Know-It-Alls who specialize in publicly discussing other people's weight problems in a derogatory and belittling manner that leaves the victim totally humiliated. "Emily, that dress looks awfully tight on you, I'll suggest you wear a dress like that after your weight loss program." In doing so, some Know-It-Alls might think the public humiliation is a "motivating pitch" to motivate the other person to work on losing weight. Sometimes the motivation for such behavior may include drawing attention to the fact that they, as Know-It-Alls, work hard to keep their weight under control. Of course, there are the Know-It-Alls who "know" all about what needs to be done to control body weight or shed excess weight. They typically have all kinds of regimens and remedies, both the clinically proven ones and the personally contrived ones. Knowing these remedies is not sufficient. At times they will browbeat others with an avalanche of knowledge, intimidating them into trying out the self-prescribed remedies and other concoctions.

Fashion

Know-It-Alls who specialize in fashion usually take the phrase "fashion police" too literal. They see themselves as the avant-garde of what is acceptable fashion-wise, even when this is no more than their personal taste and take on fashion. But then, they would not have declared themselves "fashion police" if they did not "know" all about fashion and all that you should do to look good and or look like them. Such Know-It-Alls sometimes take it upon themselves to call out and humiliate people who they think are not dressed according to their perceived acceptable standard of dressing for the occasion in question. Clearly, there is appropriate dressing for every place and occasion, but Know-It-Alls take it further, they add their spin and take on it, and disparage others who don't live up to their uppity standards. Sometimes the put down is done behind the victims back. For example, a friend of theirs says: "Mrs. Smith over there looks gorgeous today." The Know-It-All then replies: "No, not really. A red hat would have looked better than the dark red hat she is wearing. Besides her red shoes are too loud, they should have been dark red. No fashion sense, I guess?" As if it makes any difference in the darkness once the lights are dimmed and the event begins!

Current Affairs or News

Today, news worthy events happening in any part of the world can be broadcast live or relayed as news almost instantly. This preponderance of news artifacts is a fodder for Know-It-Alls who specialize in current affairs or news. They may spend hours absorbing such information after which they locate an audience, of one or many persons, to offload the information. Laden with such information it becomes difficult for them to have a civil conversation without side tracking the conversation to a continuous stream of current affairs they had read about. Or even worse still, engender a one-sided monopolistic conversation, where they are the shining stars or the "greatest" and "smartest" guy in the vicinity. Generally, such a Know-It-All will move from one news topic to the other, while their victims suffer through the knowledge dissemination or offload session. Even when a conversation is possible with them, such a Know-It-All may present their acquired knowledge in a condescending manner to humiliate those who don't "know" or who are not up to date from a current affairs point of view.

Science and Technology

Truly knowledgeable science and technology experts generally enthrall their audience in very respectful interactive conversations. They disseminate knowledge in a very controlled and limited quantity, in the correct doses if you will, so they don't overwhelm their audience with unnecessary details. They listen to responses and feedbacks from their audience and so adjust the level of detail accordingly. Know-It-Alls who specialize in science and technology actually have the opposite effect. It is almost as if there is an ardent desire to drench or plunk down information on their victim, with the net effect being that their victim feels overwhelmed or even bamboozled. Furthermore, when such Know-It-Alls have a hard time reading body language, they may mistake the silence or capitulation of the victim as acceptance of their manner of disseminating knowledge and possibly delve deeper into the subject, disseminating ever larger quantities as the conversation gradually becomes monopolistic and one-sided. Since they consider the victims inferior, they most likely will not listen to their comments. Most Know-It-Alls that specialize in this arena have the knowledge, but the manner in which they disseminate the knowledge and perhaps the desire to assert themselves as someone who "knows" the subject mentally distances them from their overwhelmed victims.

Trivia

Trivia can be very exciting when played among friends or family. In fact, it sometimes does liven up the atmosphere at get-togethers. Know-It-Alls who specialize in trivia can occasionally take it too far when they try to engage everyone they see in their favorite trivia. Very often, trivia questions are injected into conversations to test how "smart" the victim is in the Know-It-All's opinion. The problem starts when the victim cannot answer the question and the Know-It-All floods the victim with more questions to further humiliate the victim or demonstrate the Know-It-All's "superior" intellect. Repeatedly exposing a loved one to such knowledge intimidating sessions could cause emotional harm and or lack of self esteem.

Personal Dirt

Personal dirt as used here implies personal, private, intimate, positive, negative, harmful, upbuilding, confidential, entrusted, secret, etc. information about a friend, relative, loved one or even a public figure. Know-It-Alls who specialize in gathering and using personal dirt possibly get a kick out of the shock and humiliation their victims feel when they regurgitate the accumulated embarrassing knowledge and fling it in the victims face or spread it out in public to maximize the impact. Such Know-It-Alls sometimes become all attentive at the wisp of gossip or character assassination or any conversation that has personal dirt in it. In this mode they will pry and drill for more "knowledge." In a confiding conversation with a victim, they will create the impression of being all ears, caring and attentive while they gather "knowledge."

For Know-It-Alls who specialize in gathering and using personal dirt, the well worn cliché "No smoke without fire" may take on the more significant meaning that gossips are either true or have truthful and usable elements in it. Hence, the tendency to believe the worst about their friends, relatives, loved ones and public figures becomes part of their thinking process and repertoire, as they preoccupy themselves with the raunchy negative aspects of whatever they hear.

Politics

Politics is possibly one of the most controversial [1] subjects to bring up in a conversation. Perhaps because everybody has an opinion and they are entitled to their opinions. Know-It-Alls who specialize in politics are very much like those who specialize in current affairs and news in that they spend large amounts of time daily gathering political tidbits, statistics and facts. If they kept this research to themselves, or presented them in appropriate places before opportune audiences it will be fine. However, at times Know-It-Alls who specialize in politics will corner a victim in a regular conversation and barrage them with their opinions and refuse to listen to the victims opinions; quickly forgetting that the victim is also entitled to an opinion. Most often, this may lead to a prolonged argument, that escalates to the point where the Know-It-All is doggedly determined to prove their opinion is the "right" one or that they "know" more about politics than the victim.

Diet

An appropriate combination of food and drinks that meet our daily nutritional requirements, plus other healthy habits and exercise generally is everybody's goal. Clearly, it is not always easy to meet and exceed our daily nutritional requirements as well as the appropriate exercise recommendations. Now, have you ever met Know-It-Alls who specialize in diet conversations? Is it not interesting how, invariably, conversations with them resort or shift to diets or supplements or nutritional tidbits. Very often, diet Know-It-Alls are not just telling you their diet idea, they are pushing their diet idea, possibly because they "know" it will be good for you. When you sneeze around them, they "know" just the right supplement you need to "fix" the sneeze. When you clear your throat, they "know" what vitamins are missing from your meal and just where to get the untainted "natural" tablets of the vitamin. Or perhaps they have an herbal mixture that will "fix" the clearing of your throat and if you cannot find the mixture, don't worry they have it growing in their backyard garden! In this pushy mode, a victim who is constantly around them may become nervous, and rightly so, since these supplement recommendations are most often unproven or not approved by the appropriate governmental agencies.

Race

Race, like politics is one of the most controversial subjects to bring up in a conversation even among people of the same race. Naturally, everyone has an opinion and an angle about the subject. People are entitled to their opinions, since they are just that, opinions. For Know-It-Alls who specialize in race conversations, other people's balanced opinions typically are dismissed, while their opinions are promoted to the exclusion of evidence to support their opinions. This type of close minded and sometimes one-sided conversation usually makes victims who choose to be objective and neutral feel very uncomfortable. Daily or regular exposure to Know-It-Alls who specialize in race conversations could very well be emotionally draining for such victims. For some of these Know-It-Alls, exaggeration of incidents, comments, statistics and so on is more the norm than the exception in their conversations. Some of them usually will "know" some obscure scientific research or historical fact or political fact that only "they" read a while back that buttresses their flawed argument.

Gender

Gender as used here is to generally differentiate between male and female persons. For most people this classification is no different than say night or day, which is used for describing and establishing a reference frame in a conversation. Such balanced and appropriate usage does not confer superiority or inferiority, nor does it debase any gender. For Know-It-Alls who specialize in gender, frequently their conversation is polarized into male and female, with their preferred gender being conferred with superiority and the other gender being relegated to an inferior position, tacitly or blatantly. Their comments or statements generally reflect dichotomous views about gender that attempts to create the idea that they are "experts" on the subject of either gender, though most likely the one considered inferior. So then, you will frequently hear statements like "Men always..." or "Women always..." prefacing every other statement they make in a patronizing and discourteous manner. As if they "know" more about any gender than the person they are addressing. Strictly speaking, how many things are there "really" that "Women always..." that "Men don't always..."? Such Know-It-Alls may not hesitate to talk contemptuously, talk brashly or even refuse to speak to the gender they feel is inferior, with the sole intent, wittingly or unwittingly, of denigrating and subjugating the victim.

Sports

Today, you can watch literally any major sporting event live, regardless of its location. There are major television and or radio networks and channels that carry the event live, and there are numerous websites that provide live feed in real time. Even if you are not in a position to watch the sport live, updates can be streamed to your home page, cell phone as email or even as a text message. Therefore, you can follow by television, radio, internet on your home computer or internet on your mobile laptop or cell phone. For Know-It-Alls who specialize in sports, just like current affairs or news, sports data, statistics and so forth is always a click away. Some Know-It-Alls will spend hours soaking up the latest on either their favorite sport or sport in general. Brimming with a glut of sports data and information, such Know-It-Alls may seek an audience to offload all they "know" or play sports trivia. The human tendency sometimes, when such Know-It-Alls have so much information that is current and time sensitive is to monopolize conversations so they can explain and "mentally offload" all that they know. This frequently leads to such Know-It-Alls dominating the conversation, rejecting input since they "know" what they read in their research. Heated arguments and debates can also erupt when an opposing opinion is perceived as challenging the credibility of the Know-It-All who specializes in sports. Most often a denigrating form of "thrash talk" will not be too far behind.

Sexuality

Have you ever met someone whose conversations frequently had a sexual connotation or undertone? These sexual overtones in their conversation quickly turn raunchy the moment they perceive interest or that there is a listening ear. It is almost as if they have an "alternative" vocabulary of words with double meanings, innuendos, phrases with sexual overtures, vulgarity laced with humor and so forth that spews out nonstop. Your comments or statements to them are parsed and diced in search of words and phrases in their vocabulary of double meanings. There response to your comment will depend on their perceived sexual content of your expression. Know-It-Alls who specialize in sexuality tend to come across as just described. They have a morbid fascination with vocalized and suggestive sexual conversation, such that their victims feel disconcerted or completely offended. They have to let their victims "know" about the sexual content or relationship with expressions in their conversation. The discomfort around Know-It-Alls who specialize in sexuality does not stem from just talking responsibly and appropriately about sex, but the pervasive manner in which it dominates their thoughts and conversation is what unnerves their victims.

Internet

The internet and the technologies it has enabled, has without doubt changed our lives, especially since the commencement of the twenty first century. Today, phone calls cost a fraction of what they used to cost per minute. We can communicate a lot faster and receive responses a lot faster than in yesteryears. Most people use the internet for research, for leisure, for communication and so on. Know-It-Alls who specialize in internet conversations would seem to see the internet as a panacea of sorts. It is not just that they use the internet for research like everyone else but it is as if they see and get more out of it than others. So then when someone asks: "How do you know ..." the invariable response starts with: "I saw it on the internet..." Asked: "Where can I find a gas station around your apartment?" Their response starts with: "Are you logged onto the web right now...?" Similarly, their conversations are dominated to a disproportional extent with internet based activities from forums, chat rooms, social networks, message boards, etc. If they have not seen or heard about something on the internet that is probably grounds for a serious debate and or argument. Sound arguments or opinions that cannot be readily verified on the internet may be dismissed as not being plausible. Fantastic stories bandied about on unscrupulous internet websites tend to embody the gist of their conversations. They will not hesitate to leave a conversation in other to do a quick argument winning web search. Obviously, the web search and the internet usage are not the issue, but the obsession and pervasive dependence on the internet to the exclusion of sound reasoning is what victims find daunting.

Business/Finance/Money

Do you know somebody who talks nonstop about business ideas, deals, stock tips, this scheme, that product? You have been acquainted with them for years and there is always that next and better scheme, the one they always call: "This is it!" Frequently, the pitch line is that you are the only person, of all your mutual friends, fortunate to be let into the special deal they "know." Of course, your other mutual friends were not good enough to make the Know-It-All's "cut", it was just you! It does not matter that you have lost money several times in their endless deals and schemes. You see them coming and you get all nervous because you know the power of their overbearing sales pitch. Typically, Know-It-Alls who specialize in business or finance or money conversations have a way of dominating the conversation and corralling their victims into a corner and then barraging or plying them with manipulative words or questions that are meant to wheedle a financial contribution or participation in their endless schemes. They also have the uncanny ability to pick victims and fasten onto them like leeches. They are leeches because most often they will return again and again, regardless of past failures and try to milk or take the victim for more. The victim's, sometimes feeble, defensive words are effortlessly discarded or rebutted as inferior or worthless or not a good enough reason to avoid investing; all the time underhandedly reassuring the victim that they "know" what is best for them.

Health

We all want good health. Even as elusive as good health might be, we normally do our best to remain relatively healthy. Besides, relatively good health means different things to different people. What one person might be content with as relatively good health may not be for another. Know-It-Alls who specialize in health conversations tend to take health consciousness to a different level. They frequently dominate conversations with health issues, and would consciously or unconsciously cajole or steer the conversation towards health issues or focus excessively on health related aspects of a conversation. They seem to know the latest procedures long before they hit the consumer market place. Sometimes they have already participated in seminars and workshops convened for the new procedures they are aggressively promoting in their conversations. Such Know-It-Alls may not hesitate to talk a victim out of a doctor recommended regimen if that can make the victim try their own regimen which they as non-doctors "know" will work for you. And why will "their" regimen not work for "you?" They "know" more than all doctors do and are "smarter" than everybody else, and that is why they are called Know-It-Alls is it not?

Computer

Do you have a friend who talks nonstop about the new computer or laptop they bought? These days, cell phones, tablets and electronic notepads can be included on the list as well since these products are faster and more power than computers of the years gone by. For some reason the new computer is sometimes located in a convenient location and as soon as you arrive you are ushered to the computer for another round of lecture on the marvels of a computer and the software they contain. Or it could be the latest cell phone apps and the amazing things it can do. Someone listening to your friend describe how documents are prepared on a computer; for example, might think that you probably prepare your own documents with a calculator or something! But then as a friend you probably sit patiently and suffer through the monopolistic one-sided lecture hoping the novelty of the computer your friend bought during the office sale will wear off soon. Some Know-It-Alls who specialize in computer conversations tend to be patronizing or condescending to their victims, presuming that the victim either knows nothing or does not have access to a computer. It does not occur to them that the victim probably has a computer and is possibly more computer literate than they are. Such Know-It-Alls also sound belittling when they have the opportunity to make public presentations. They make their presentation sound as if they are talking to or presenting to dimwits, even when they are aware that some in the audience are several eons more advanced in the use of computers for daily work activities than they are. But then, think about, if they really had solid content to present why would they waste time on trivialities or use petty details to fill out their presentation time? This exaggerated outlook of their "brilliance" is a sore spot and a source of frequent clashing in some workplaces.

Hobby

A lot of people have hobbies. These hobbies like all past time activities are meant to be relaxing. In other words, it is a thing we do for relaxation and winding down. Hobbyists frequently talk about their hobbies and are always trying to hone their hobbies. Some have even turned their hobby and the fueling passion for the hobby into successful businesses. Know-It-Alls who specialize in hobby conversations on the other hand tend to dominate and drench conversations with their hobbyist pursuits. But if they only dominated conversations and lectured about it, it will be a bit bearable for some people. However, some Know-It-Alls who specialize in hobby conversations will try to recruit more people to join them in the pursuit of their hobby and when someone declines they will frequently resort to verbal pressure as they assure the victim that they "know" it will be to their benefit. Victims backed into a corner like that, with a room full of other "Yes" people, may sooner or later under duress drop their "No" and grudgingly join the crowd.

Now that we have seen some domains or bodies of knowledge that interest Know-It-Alls, the question then is how do they manifest the Know-It-All behavior especially when they are in a conversation where there domain of interest is the theme of the conversation?

Chapter 6: Manifestations of the Know-It-All Behavior

We have defined the phrase Know-It-All and who is a Know-It-All. We have also discussed the medium and settings through which Know-It-Alls disseminate their so-called knowledge, we enumerated the types of Know-It-All and domains or bodies of knowledge that Know-It-Alls specialize in disseminating. In some of the previous chapters we also got a glimpse of how the Know-It-All behavior is manifested. In this chapter we will enumerate the different manifestations of the Know-It-All behavior distilled from the types discussed in chapter 4. In other words, we are going to talk about how Know-It-Alls come across to us or the various ways they outwardly express that they know everything. It is possible that some of them don't know that is how they come across, but nonetheless this chapter elucidates how we perceive their Know-It-All behavior. An online newsletter at itstime.com aptly describes a person difficult to deal with like a Know-It-All, saying: "… the difficult person is someone who is working from the negative side of their personality, rather than a conscious desire to be difficult.

The person is often unaware of themselves and how they affect others. They also don't realize how harmful their actions are." [1]

What does the manifestation or the outward expression of the Know-It-All behavior actually mean? To illustrate, a person identified as a verbal abuser may, through their verbal abuse, manipulate, vituperate, control and dominate their victim. The manipulation, vituperation, control and domination are the ways the verbal abuser manifests the verbal abuse. In a similar vein, Know-It-Alls might manifest the Know-It-All behavior by manipulating, vituperating, controlling and dominating a victim through the use and dissemination of their so-called knowledge. The fact that they are friends, relatives, loved ones, and co-worker, etc. of the victim does not diminish the impact of their behavior. Very often, "friendships are not always as satisfying as we would like them to be. Some can actually be poisonous, causing grief and hurt. While some of our most profound happiness is found with friends, so is some of our deepest pain." [2]

In Mike Leibling's book "How People Tick - A guide to over 50 types of difficult people and how to handle them" we can readily identify many types of people who if they are additionally Know-It-Alls would really make life difficult for their victims. The types of people listed in his book include biased people who may be close minded, bullies who may belittle and intimidate, cold people who may be insensitive, disrespectful people who may humiliate others, hostile people who may be confrontational and rude, must-have-the-last-word people, nit-picky people who may be obsessed with finding fault in others, patronizing people who may be self important, and selfish people who may be self-centered. [3] Clearly, not all bullies or all nit-picky people are Know-It-Alls; however, for bullies who are Know-It-Alls or nit-picky people who are Know-It-Alls the effect of this manifestation of their Know-It-All behavior is more impacting.

As we discussed earlier, knowledge is not the issue, neither is the mental acumen of the Know-It-All in question here, after all we need to learn and acquire knowledge from people who are truly knowledgeable, however, it is the embodiment of delivery, the ambience of delivery, the undercurrent of delivery, the impact of the delivery, the aura of the delivery that transforms the knowledge being imparted into a verbal weapon, a "knowledge bullet" that makes us perceive the Know-It-All as manifesting the Know-It-All behavior in the ways listed below. Therefore, we perceive that Know-It-Alls are:

Obsessed with corrections

Have you ever been at a social event or visiting friends or family and a Know-It-All corrected his or her spouse nonstop? The relentless [4] correction, which reminds one of water dripping noisily and annoyingly at set intervals just before your wake up time in the morning, might even, be directed at others as well. Sometimes the person being corrected gets flustered and begins to fumble in their conversation or they just stop talking. You will think that the Know-It-All will read the body language of the person being corrected and desist. No, they usually don't and that is because it is a deeply ingrained habit [5] and this habit persists even when their correction adds absolutely no value [6] to the conversation. A spouse says: "We met the Joneses at about 7pm." The Know-It-All fires the automatic correction: "No honey, it was at 6:55pm not 7pm." Of course, the ineffectual correction and the five minute difference in the Know-It-All's perspective of time will "prove" to onlookers that the Know-It-All is "detailed" with time.

Furthermore, is this social event the perfect place for the Know-It-All to let the world know that his or her spouse is not "detailed" with time? The point is that a Know-It-All's continuous corrections, perhaps to self promote their mental prowess, distracts and makes onlookers feel ill at ease and denigrates the victim. This is true even when Know-It-Alls think they are domain "experts" or "know" everything there is to know in what they are correcting. Oftentimes the correction is not just grammatical [7] but could be in any of several domains of knowledge since the intent is to prove the victim and anyone else wrong, [8] while they, the Know-It-Alls stand or "shine" as the correct ones.

An appropriate question then is; are Know-It-Alls insensitive or what? Remember that "when it is said that someone is an insensitive person this typically means that that person displays certain attitudes including a lack of awareness of the effects of his or her actions on others and a failure to care about these effects." [9] Since this is a habit formed, perhaps since childhood and over the years, it is possible that Know-It-Alls lack awareness of the impact of their actions. Or it could also be that they disregard [10] the moral and sentimental impact of their incessant corrections or the "knowledge pellets" they fire at their victim. A victim living with a Know-It-All obsessed with corrections may over time begin to dread [24, 41] social events or anywhere there is a possibility of being corrected in front of everybody. This, no doubt, could impact their life negatively. Bear in mind that there are people who live with Know-It-Alls obsessed with corrections. Here is an example of the typical way such victims usher in their day: "Honey, good morning, I still have some scrambled egg and bacon left, do you want some with coffee?" The Know-It-All rolls over, squints at the bedside clock with 12:03pm displayed, and retorts: "It's good afternoon not good morning. Should you not be talking about lunch? Scrambled eggs and bacon are for breakfast." Of course, Know-It-Alls have to start their day being "correct."

Domineering

Do you recall the last time you were with a group of friends or family members chitchatting about nothing in particular and a close friend of yours approached and respectfully asked to talk to you? Then, to your dismay and astonishment a Know-It-All friend or family member despotically dismissed your friend with the well worn: "We are busy right now…" or "We are in a meeting right now…" Suddenly, you find yourself in an awkward position because the overbearing or domineering Know-It-All friend or family member arbitrarily "knew" what was best for you at that time and authorized himself or herself to act in your "best" interest. Sometimes such Know-It-All friends or family members would actually answer questions directed to you as if you never existed or where not present; meanwhile, you are sitting right there in front of them. Of course, they already "know" your response, so why give you the dignity and respect due you by letting you answer the question directed to you.

How about the Know-It-All boss who "knows" everything except the location of an online form, and then, instead of asking you outright where it was on your company's intranet website, he will make it sound like he was actually telling you where it was? "Mary, the ABC form is not on the intranet home page." That is probably because he expects you to say: "Oh no, Mr. Know-It-All Boss, it is not on the intranet home page, give me a minute and let me email the correct link to you." But then, why would he ask Mary; that would mean he did not "know" everything he thinks a "boss" is supposed to know. Then, there is the team meeting, where a typical Know-It-All boss literally hijacks [4] team member comments and totally dominates the conversation. [11] Such Know-It-All bosses sometimes ask questions, and as the team member begins to answer, they cut the team member off and answer the question they asked. Of course, they sort of "read" the team member's mind, figured out what needs to be said and then helped the team member say it.

The expression superiority complex [12] has been used to describe people who tend to dominate conversations; hence later in this book we will see how Karl Menninger [16] defines that expression. Nonetheless, domineeringness in conversations include behaviors such as "denigrating or criticizing the other person or what they do, think, etc., bragging about oneself, verbally aggressing, arguing or negatively challenging the other person and reminding the person that they could have used the aversive stimulus [or reprimand] to hurt them." [13] Dominating conversations inevitably leads to one-sided lectures [14] or monologues and most often everybody else in the conversation is staring at the Know-It-All quietly, wondering why he or she has to dominate the conversation and lecture them in this manner. Given that some Know-It-Alls "know" what is best for their victims or beleaguered audience, they might be emboldened by the quiet audience, because they are least likely to self criticize [14] their behavior, and so continue to disseminate more knowledge from their endless reservoir of "knowledge."

Another driving factor that propels Know-It-Alls to dominate conversations is the penchant to have the last word. [15] Of course and why not, as Know-It-Alls endowed with knowledge and who "know" everything, their voice and expression should be heard last at the expense of others in the conversation, after all, they probably reason, people tend to remember what they heard last. Some Know-It-Alls will strive for this last kick in a conversation even when their last word is meaningless or adds nothing to the conversation.

Faultfinding

Think for a moment of all the faultfinders you know, not just the ones that "know" everything. Is it not true that they share that same habitual disapproval of whatever is presented to them? It does not matter what it is. "Joe Doe wrote a wonderful article in the Local Gazette." "No, not from the way he signed off on that article, he should have put his full name instead of JD." "What a good job Angela did here, the gymnasium floor for the first time is spotless." "Yeah, I really wish she had not used the cheap brand of detergent." "Are you going to Martha's baby shower?" "You know, I don't know. I think a third kid is one too many." It reminds you of a Woodpecker pecking out faults, does it not? These Know-It-Alls seem to always have something they "know" about the victim that must be used to deprecate or denigrate the victim.

Sometimes, the faultfinding could be as a result of the victim not meeting their "standard" or level of expectation based on the "knowledge" they have acquired over the years on the subject matter. In other words, they "know" everything about how it should have been done, but the victim, unfortunately, has not met that "standard." In conversations with such Know-It-Alls it is more or less as if their minds are minesweepers, sweeping the conversation, looking for potential flaws to exploit and deprecate. Alfred Adler relates this proclivity to faultfinding [17] and deprecating to vain and ambitious people who in their quest to shine or be admired as the "best" and the "greatest" may belligerently injure other people with their words. Of course, when Know-It-Alls find fault in everyone around them, since they know everything, then, their "brilliance" will rise from the ashes and "shine" for all to see, even when their malevolent words tear down their victim emotionally and hurt their victim just as much as physical blows. [18]

But seriously, is it not true that finding fault and tearing down is a lot easier than building someone else up? For example, in the examples above, imagine how long it took Angela to mop and polish the gymnasium floor. Now, compare that with the fact that within a few seconds, the Know-It-All, who "knows" a better detergent, disparaged and relegated Angela's work as not being "good" enough because she supposedly used a cheap detergent. What the Know-It-All did not know was that the person having the conversation with her actually bought the detergent and not Angela. This brings us to the question; are Know-It-Alls who find fault in other people hiding behind the lack of original contribution to a conversation, by finding faults and using those as crutches to prop up their noncreative contributions?

Condescending

Do you have a Know-It-All in your life who is obsessed with writing down "detailed" instructions on a piece of paper for almost everything he or she wants you to do or that you are expected to do? Such Know-It-Alls would sometimes insist on a list with two items on it, even when you have assured them that you remember the two items that need to be picked up at the store. Imagine for a moment that you took the Know-It-All to a casual meeting with your business associates of many years. At the end of the meeting, you are assigned one action item by your business associates, and you remember the action item very well, but then the Know-It-All hands you an unsolicited list containing fifteen items he "thinks" should be your action items.

Consider the condescending Know-It-All co-worker who "knows" everything in your workplace and beyond. The boss asks her to spend ten minutes with you and show you a process with three easy steps. One hour later, the Know-It-All is still describing trivial unrelated stuff in a condescending tone that leaves no doubt about what she thinks of you. Meanwhile, you have no idea if you have covered the three steps or not. Such Know-It-Alls could sometimes literally insist that you write down every trivial and worthless "detail" they have "taught" you. Of course, you must take notes given that your life could depend on those trivial and worthless details! These examples illustrate how some Know-It-Alls can, in the name of showing you how "detailed" they are and how detailed "you" should be, talk and act in a condescending manner. The list and the details are not the problems here, after all, we need lists and details from time to time, it is the fact that they are unsolicited and or the victim finds it embarrassing, humiliating and condescending.

Another effective variation of this Know-It-All behavior that Know-It-Alls use frequently is "condescending superiority" [19] sometimes aimed at the victims they perceive as "inferior" to them, especially intellectually. Perhaps, by acting or talking in a condescending [20] manner, Know-It-Alls hope to rub in the fact that they are intellectually "superior" and are doing the victims a favor by condescending to their level to address them or even have a conversation. Why not?

"They like to communicate as if they are talking to a child." [21] Sometimes, this condescending air of superiority is based simply on a bloated sense of entitlement [22] and not on any real abilities of the Know-It-All. What other message is the Know-It-All conveying by their condescending air of superiority? "They make it clear that they have a low opinion of you by the condescending way they deal with you. They ask for your opinion, then ignore your ideas, interrupt you or zap you with putdowns as they dismiss your suggestions. Their distorted high opinion of themselves encourages them to degrade and devalue others." [23]

Projecting flaws and self criticism onto others

From time to time we see parents who will not allow their preteen child participate in activities like reciting a poem or making a public presentation in front of an audience. Why? Because the Know-It-All parents "know" the child will be embarrassed or ashamed or may not remember the poem or presentation. Or they might claim their children are too young to make such public appearances. The list of excuses could be longer. Meanwhile, we know lots of preteen children, same age or younger, who successfully recite poems and make public presentations. How about the Know-It-All co-worker who is confident it will take you at least three weeks to learn a new process because it took him two weeks? But then, to their chagrin it takes you less than a week to learn the process and come up to speed.

What is happening in these scenarios we mentioned in the above paragraph? "The tendency to criticize is deeply embedded in the controlling person's character. Basically, he [or she] projects his [or her] self-criticism onto others." [25] That is the point. Do you remember the Know-It-Alls who have a condescending way of shoving a list into your hand for the most trivial of things? Could the real problem be that they have a hard time remembering things without a formal list to guide them? This is probably the reason they assume that their loved ones or friends must also need an unsolicited list to remember two items or a few items that typically don't require a list.

What is projecting? "Projection may be defined as the tendency to attribute falsely to other people motives or traits that are our own, or that in some way explain or justify our own [motives]." [26] As humans, we have the inherent proclivity to project [27] onto others things we feel we might not do well or things that are uncertain or things we are scared about or things that are vague about ourselves. These may include our own intimate flaws or things we frequently criticize ourselves about. Consequently, we may assume everybody has the same failings like us. Knowing that we have this penchant is fine, since we can work to curb it. However, it would seem that some Know-It-Alls have a harder time curbing this tendency to project [28] their flaws and self criticism onto others, perhaps because they feel they "know" everything, and so if they are having a hard time accomplishing a goal, then, automatically, everyone else is also incapable of accomplishing the goal.

Manipulative and controlling

History is replete with humans who have used manipulation and control to achieve their selfish and personal ambitions. Today, manipulation continues to be a powerful tool in the hands of manipulators. Manipulation is perhaps more potent in the hand of a Know-It-All who has spent more time studying and accumulating intimate details, personal weaknesses and flaws of his or her victim, in addition to the general knowledge about the victim's personal tastes and likes. This enables the Know-It-All to appear very "smart" from the point of view of the victim.

Take for example John and Julie. They are dating. John has no job and practically mooches of Julie every time they go out shopping or to dinner or anywhere, in fact, the car John drives is Julie's car. This particular evening, John arrives with his friends to pick Julie up and take her to a grocery store in a shopping strip. Julie had reluctantly come along to buy John his toiletries since she was trying to save up for her rent. After buying John's toiletries in the grocery store, John casually strolls into the video game store next door, so does Julie and John's friends. Soon, John has Julie corralled in a corner, while he extols the features of a video game he and Julie always wanted and how Julie could demonstrate her love one more time by, of course, buying the video game. John quickly dismisses Julie's pleas of saving for her rent and reminds her that cash is not needed since she can use her credit card, a credit card that is already in default and nearly maxed out. Like all the times before this particular evening Julie obliges.

While it may be obvious that the whole ruse about going to the grocery store was primarily to manipulate or wheedle Julie into buying the video game, the disturbing part is the fact that John was using his "knowledge" of Julie's weakness and her love for video games. Manipulative and controlling people use manipulation to alter the outcome of events so the person being manipulated will act in a predetermined [29] way, or "to prevent you from making a choice, to feel in control and powerful, to impose their reality on you ... to distort reality, to diminish you." [30] It is not difficult to imagine

John telling his cronies later that he "knew" Julie would buy the video game; he just had to "play" it right.

Know-It-Alls, who use their knowledge to manipulate and control others, can also manipulate a group or groups of people to achieve their goal of denigrating or disparaging a victim. For example, such Know-It-Alls could create a fake profile page on a social networking site and then drawing on their knowledge of what the likes and dislikes of the victim are, they can populate the fake profile page and then insert their offensive insinuations and derogatory content. Next, they will select a group or groups of people who know the victim and then directly or covertly publicize the fake profile page. The manipulative intent works when people lured to the fake profile page react as the Know-It-Alls expected.

Know-It-Alls can be very controlling [58] and often exercise such control by being manipulative as highlighted above and domineering [13] as was discussed in detail in the section "Domineering" above. In this controlling mode the Know-It-All literally becomes a director or commander of the victim's affairs. Often the reason for such Know-It-All behavior is "to feel in control and powerful." [30] This perhaps is because the Know-It-All wants to be sure the victim is doing everything "right" and as "directed." The "right" here meaning what the Know-It-All "knows" is best for the victim based on his or her "knowledge" of the victim and his or her grandiose allusion to knowing everything. In the next chapter control will be discussed further to show the effect of this Know-It-All behavior on the victim.

Hypercritical

Constructive criticism, when used in a balanced manner and in the appropriate setting, can be very helpful, as it gently and palatably exposes flaws that need to be mended. Though criticism is a synonym of faultfinding, discussed earlier, it is appropriate to give the hypercritical manifestation of the Know-It-All behavior a different section since this is criticism taken to the extreme. Criticism is "making a negative evaluation of the other person, her [or his] actions, or attitudes. [For example:] "You brought it on yourself – you've got nobody else to blame for the mess you are in.""" [31] Hence, in hypercriticism the negative evaluation is frequent and extreme enough to cause the victim emotional harm and hurt. In the example cited above, it is easy to see how knowledge of the victims mess and circumstances is being used by the person criticizing to further hurt the victim who is already in a mess.

Know-It-Alls, who hypercriticize incessantly, probably do so because they feel they have a "smarter", faster and better idea [31] than their victim and so use the excessive criticism to exercise power [32] over their victim. Unfortunately, the poignant thing about such extreme criticism is that it is verbal abuse [33] and the precursor to physical violence. [34]

Perhaps one of the most difficult things to comprehend when Know-It-Alls use their self appointed position as critic and their assumed "superior" knowledge to incessantly criticize their victim is the fact that most often Know-It-Alls have glaring character flaws that are easily overlooked by their victim. Have you ever seen or possibly heard a seriously obese man constantly, like a hammer, tell his slightly overweight wife that she needs to lose weight immediately? Such men would actually proceed to list all they "know" their wife should do to lose weight and all she should do not to gain weight. And, most often this is not being said in the privacy of their home only, but in public as well, perhaps to see how effective the humiliation factor will be. It is even more surprising to learn that some of the most intense [35] feelings, in this case negative feelings, are directed towards those closest to us, be they friends or relatives or love ones.

Pompous

Pompous or magniloquent people have an exaggerated [36] opinion of themselves or a "distorted high opinion" [23] of themselves, and an urgent need to be the center of attention and the "shine" in private and in public. It is not surprising then that pomposity figures prominently in the definition of a Know-It-All as we saw earlier. There are many reasons why a person could feel pompous; one of them is when someone presumptuously thinks they "know" more than anybody else about whatever subject matter, or actually that they "know" everything. Perhaps, you have or have had a friend who talks nonstop about how all the women at work want him, how the new female boss could not resist him and so took him to lunch; even though there were twelve other team members who went to the monthly team lunch, how a beautiful and charming workmate finally asked for his phone number today; even though it turns out she was updating the department home phone list, how an executive vice president came down to the mail room specifically to beg him to make copies, and after he made the copies, the executive vice president begged him not to leave the company, since they would hate to lose a good photocopier like him and other morose tales such pompous Know-It-Alls narrate.

Of course, we need not forget about important Jane. Her company today threw a huge midday bash for her, to honor her enrollment at a Community College Continuous Education program; even though all she received was a casual mention in the middle of a boring send off speech by the company president for another executive officer. Of course, there was the after party during which, due to her popularity, a few big execs suddenly started to flirt with her, naturally they wanted her, but she did not want them; even though all that happened was her boss' boss shook her hand warmly and congratulated her for enrolling in the continuous education program. Oh, one more thing, how the company gave her a one-time cash card for a popular restaurant and she already charged up a storm on the card; even though all that happened was that her boss let her take home as much leftover food as she wanted. Sure, the food was from the popular restaurant she mentioned.

Could this outlandish take on self opinion be due to an elusive obsession with perfection? In other words, the obsession with perfection [37] makes Know-It-Alls lose their sense of proportion and they end up acting and expressing themselves, in a self-important make believe or like Alfred Adler described such power hungry individuals, they will express themselves in "a larger-than-life personality ideal". [38] This preoccupation with self or pomposity is one of the reasons narcissism is often associated with Know-It-Alls.

Even when such Know-It-Alls are narrating an event that happened or a goal they achieved, typically the fundamentals of the narration is to draw attention [39] to themselves and show how "smart" or how "great" or how whatever they feel will make them "shine." The fixation or penchant to shine in turn impels the Know-It-

All to do whatever is possible to maintain the "shine" status quo, including subtly or aggressively countering and negating other peoples' views, opinions, thoughts, comments, feelings, believes and generally being disagreeable to any opposing view.

Exaggerating

In our life time we have or will probably run into people who exaggerate a lot of things they say. An accident with twelve people wounded becomes an accident where dozens died. A weather forecast with a slight possibility of showers becomes an impending thunderstorm. A convenience store heist where three thousand dollars was stolen while six people are in the store becomes a hostage situation where six people are taken hostage and the ransom demanded was three thousand dollars. Then there is Uncle Anthony at the playground with his little nieces and nephews and they ask him what Pontchartrain on his T-Shirt means since he carries himself as the family "encyclopedia" and famed for his internet conversations. He is nowhere near a web browser, nor does he own a Smartphone, but he has an idea it has something to do with New Orleans, so he tells the kids it is a train service in New Orleans that runs between two train stations Pont and Char.

Most often when a Know-It-All exaggerates or overstates a fact it is out of a dishonest sense of duty, that is, the necessity to keep up the appearance of someone who "knows" or someone who is admired for their "great" mental prowess. As if saying: "I don't know" will make them any less knowledgeable, but then, would that not be owning up that there was something they don't know, perhaps that is why they exaggerate.

Such Know-It-Alls don't only exaggerate their knowledge on trivial facts, statistics and so on, but sometimes on things that can be very damaging. Take for example the Know-It-All who tells a woman that her husband was having an intimate conversation with another woman in a grocery store café; they were holding hands the Know-It-All claims. A week later, the same story, now told to another person, a mutual friend of theirs, had morphed into making out in a car outside in the parking lot. By the time the scandalous exaggeration is sorted out by the woman and her husband, it turns out the Know-It-All actually saw the woman's husband having a casual non-amorous conversation with the checkout clerk while checking out at the grocery store.

When anybody including Know-It-Alls exaggerate so frequently, it becomes very difficult to take them serious [40] since often there is no way to know if they are stating facts or just living up to the reputation of someone who is supposed to "know."

An Unsolicited spokesperson

Does it not feel strange when a Know-It-All intervenes, unsolicited, to answer questions directed at you, while you are seated [45] or are standing right there? Besides they do this frequently and in different settings and are not just answering everyday trivial questions. They are answering much more serious personal questions. For example, such Know-It-Alls, unsolicited, will not hesitate to explain to the waiter what "you" want to drink and eat or explain to another person details about "your" illness or broadcast the problems "you" are having on your job or marriage or relationship and above all, to your embarrassment. It is almost as if you don't exist [49] at that moment or that the Know-It-All "knows" precisely what your thoughts are and what you would have said and then the Know-It-All voices it for you like a spokesperson, as if speaking on behalf of a child. The presumptuous intervention is strange because the Know-It-All's unsolicited response is completely different from what your response would have been. So then, you are torn between correcting the unsolicited response immediately and making the Know-It-All look imprudent for their intervention or letting the faux pas slide for the moment.

In situations like the above, the Know-It-All unsolicited spokesperson only succeeds in depriving others from knowing the victim's thoughts and feelings about the conversation at hand or question asked. For people in relationships where they have to be with such a Know-It-All often, it can be a daunting task maintaining their identity separate and distinct from the usurping Know-It-All who "knows" everything including their victim's personal thoughts and opinions. Know-It-Alls who tend to act as unsolicited spokespersons often have a propensity to hold monopolistic and one-sided conversations. How?

Such monopolistic and one sided conversation sometimes results when Know-It-Alls are too concerned with their own agenda or point, [42] what they are about to say and the "knowledge" they are about to disseminate. In that mode, they are likely warding off what they feel is a challenge to the spotlight. As if their knowledge will disappear if they let others contribute to the conversation. But then, it could be that they are too self absorbed [43] to notice that others are not contributing to the conversation and that it is inappropriate to carry on an unbalanced [43] conversation. Perhaps, it is the desire to show off [44] whatever "knowledge" they have, that engenders the desire to monopolize the conversation.

Prone to lies

Prone to lies as used here is distinctly different from someone who exaggerates the truth or facts or someone who has misspoken. Prone to lies as used here refers to situations where a Know-It-All knowingly speaks a false statement with the intent to mislead and enhance a knowledge dissemination session in their favor. For example, Know-It-Alls who are prone to lies and who frequent forums, chat rooms and have profiles on social networking sites are more likely than not to post or type information that is false and or clearly deceptive.

Take the case of social network profile photos; how many times have you heard of people who carried on online relationships with someone and when they eventually met, the profile photos bore no semblance to the person they were carrying on the relationship with? It turns out; it was a friend's photo! Of course, as a Know-It-All he probably regaled his victim with lies he "knows" will fit the false profile photo and what he perceives his victim expects to hear. How about Know-It-All pedophiles who lie by pretending to be teenagers when in reality they are grandfathers? Then, with their "knowledge" of what teenagers do and what is currently popular with teenagers they craftily and detrimentally exploit their victim. Meanwhile, during all this interaction with the teenager, the Know-It-All pedophile is gathering personal information with guile and disseminating the "knowledge" he feels his victim wants to see or hear or learn in the frequent chat conversations or online interactions.

The online arena is not the only medium through which Know-It-Alls prone to lies disseminate their tainted knowledge; they deploy their gambit also in bold faced lies [46] told in daily conversations to make them shine and prop up the image that they "know" everything. Most often, these Know-It-Alls are persons considered to be very "knowledgeable" by their victims and so they take advantage of their reputation to fabricate very colorful lies when the truth does not fit. Such Know-It-Alls pick their victims very carefully and such victims tend to be persons who adore them and who have an ear for tales, both true and false; victims they can bulldoze with a few facts laced with lies in an amalgam of deceit that the victim helps to spread or acts on.

Take for an example a Know-It-All stockbroker who has collected money from friends and family who entrust him with all their life's savings. With time the investments the Know-It-All stockbroker made began to go awry and lose money heavily. An honest stockbroker will honestly inform his investors and try to work towards recovery. Not so with the Know-It-All stockbroker who is prone to lies, and who thinks that friends and family see him as the "greatest" stockbroker in recent memory and the "brightest" of all money managers. So, the Know-It-All stockbroker resorts to forging and printing fake monthly or quarterly statements, with all the associated subterfuges necessary to keep alive the deception and lies. The Know-It-All stockbroker probably goes this far in deception to maintain the status quo of someone who "knows" everything about stock broking and the financial markets.

Know-It-Alls who are prone to telling lies use confabulations [47] to justify self serving and unsupportable opinions or views, in other words, the Know-It-All is convinced that the lie is the truth, of course, as long as it serves his or her primary purpose of deceiving.

Overly assertive

Have you ever had a conversation with a Know-It-All and the more you tried to yield in an argument or conversation that has gone south, the more aggressive, louder and forceful he or she became? Even in this state of acquiescing for the sake of peace and some quiet, the Know-It-All does not get it and is still on the warpath firing more "knowledge bullets" at you to buttress and "drive" home their unsubstantiated point. Such Know-It-Alls tend to be overly assertive and deliberately read attempts to bring peace and order to a conversation as a sign of weakness that emboldens their aggression. In other words, the attempts to yield and seek a peaceful resolution to the escalating argument are seen as positive indications that they are "right" and you are "wrong" or may be that they "know" everything of course and you just tacitly admitted you don't know anything, at least not as much as them.

While assertion can be a positive quality that helps you "to maintain respect, satisfy your needs, and defend your rights," [48] it is distinctly different from being overly assertive like an overly assertive Know-It-All, whose assertion includes elements of aggression, "dominating, manipulating, abusing or controlling others." [48] Additionally, the Know-It-All's unusually high degree of certainty [49] about his or her ideas, opinions [44] and views, that fuels the overly assertive behavior, can be overwhelmingly intimidating for a victim.

Another facade to some overly assertive Know-It-Alls is a tendency to be just as demanding as they are assertive. For example, you promised an overly assertive Know-It-All friend that you will give her your car to go shopping at 3pm on a Saturday. The Know-It-All, of course, "knows" you will be home all day Saturday and changes her plan to 12noon without consulting you and then arrives at 12noon expecting you to drop your 12noon plans so she can drive off with your car. And, no, she is not asking politely, she is demanding and reminds you that she already "knows" you don't go anywhere on Saturday, that is why she made the plans without consulting you. It does not matter what reasons or viewpoints you present, like: it is your car and you have a life, those are quickly dismissed and the vehicle demanded ever more urgently, if not aggressively. Those are the type of Know-It-Alls who constantly preface every other statement with: "I already know that..." When it is obvious from their blunders, indiscretions and lapses in judgment that they are stone cold clueless!

Self-centered

A self-centered person has herself or himself as the center of interest. This reminds one of a revolving door that everyone must pass through and continue on while the revolving door remains intact and in the same position. It is more or less as if a self-centered person's first thought process in mundane activities is: "Folks, what's in it for me?" or "You need me but I don't need you." That seems to be the thought process, even when they need others. Know-It-Alls who are self-centered would tend to use their "knowledge" to influence things to give them an undue or selfish advantage or to consistently serve their personal interest.

Have you ever seen Know-It-Alls who are self-centered organize a get-together? Often the Know-It-All will start organization of such a get-together by asking if he or she could use your place. Most probably that is alright with you since you have ample room and time for the get-together. The Know-It-All then assures you that food and drinks are all taken care of and you relax. On the get-together day, as the guests arrive, the guests bring the assorted food and drink required for the get-together and before long there is abundant food and drink for all. This is wonderful, except it then dawns on you that the Know-It-All brought and contributed nothing. All the Know-It-All did was use her "knowledge" of who could bring what and then cunningly assigned everyone something to bring or do. Of course, just before the get-together starts, that is when you realize it was a get-together organized by the Know-It-All to send off the Know-It-All's cousin to college. Something the Know-It-All never mentioned or revealed to you!

Have you met self-centered Know-It-Alls who "know" all the expensive restaurants when you offer to take them out to dinner? They not only "know" the expensive restaurants, they will cajole you towards one of them and order up a storm; as they try out menu items they read about on the "internet." Of course, they have to put their "knowledge" to work. Now, when such Know-It-Alls ask you out, they swiftly draw down on their wealth of "knowledge" and remember restaurants with buffet servings for a fixed price, and by the way, these are buffets you frequent for their moderate prices.

Given that it is all about self, such Know-It-Alls will flaunt [51] their abilities and prowess [39] at the most indiscrete moments, if the end result will be to "shine" or confirm to their victim and or onlookers that they "know." Such self promotion and showy display of knowledge may sound justified to a Know-It-All who actually has knowledge on the subject matter, even when their victims feel overwhelmed, [39] uncomfortable, intimidated and sometimes humiliated by the way the "knowledge bullets" are fired at them in a condescending manner. This self promotion is furthermore carried on with exuberance and confidence that comes from a long period of promoting [52] themselves as a way of propping up their popularity.

Obnoxious

An obnoxious person is "annoying or objectionable due to being a showoff or attracting undue attention to oneself." [53] This definition of the word obnoxious helps us see why some Know-It-Alls can be described as obnoxious. The Know-It-All is not just self promoting or showing off like we discussed in the last section, but the effect is annoying, detestable and objectionable. Do you recall any of your friends whom you have absolutely no problem identifying as a Webster Know-It-All? This Know-It-All is really smart [54] and does know a lot of "stuff." The only problem is that in public settings the indiscretion in the form of "knowledge" that spews out of this Know-It-All's mouth makes you want to reach out and surgically staple the mouth shut until you leave the vicinity.

So imagine for a minute that one day, you take this Know-It-All to a relative of yours who was paralyzed from a football accident some years ago. You ring the bell and just as the door opens swiftly, this Know-It-All, looking all around, blurts out: "It looks like a cripple or invalid lives here. What are those ramps for?" The stinging humiliation in front of your relative would leave much to be desired. Would it not?

Then, there is the visit to your aunt whose last son has a slight speech impediment. The Know-It-All who fames himself as a kid lover takes it upon himself to play with your aunt's son and then you hear him say: "Why are you staring at me that way? I just asked a simple question. Are you dumb or something?" As usual you stride over and save the situation. Next, your aunt serves a dish the Know-It-All had never seen before, but it looks similar to another dish the Know-It-All had eaten elsewhere. The Know-It-All launches into a lecture of how your aunt's cooking is bland in comparison to the similar dish he had eaten elsewhere. Of course, you cut him off and save the situation. But it is unending. Your uncle has a cough and has discretely covered his mouth with a napkin each time he coughed. Out of the blue, the Know-It-All blurts out to your aunt's son: "Stay away from your dad, before you catch his Pertussis." Again, you step in and explain to your aunt's son that dad has a cough and not a whooping cough.

Without doubt, knowledge can be used obnoxiously and knowledge in the head of obnoxious [19] Know-It-Alls with such impetuous dispositions is like someone carrying around a loaded gun with a faulty trigger and or safety catch. Those "knowledge bullets" will "sneak" off the barrel mouth from time to time, to the humiliation and embarrassment of all around.

Obsessed with perfection in words, thoughts and deeds

Know-It-Alls who are obsessed with perfection in words, thoughts and deeds most often lose touch with reality and in that "grip of neurotic perfectionism ... will think that [they are] by nature more orderly and accurate than others." [37] Why should such wishful thinking be labeled a fallacy? Because even a cursory examination of the Know-It-All's life frequently reveals flaws, indiscretions, poor decisions and sometimes profound weaknesses just like in the average populace. In insisting that their opinions or preferences are superior, such Know-It-Alls wittingly or unwittingly confuse [22] their preferences with perfection. In doing so, they advertently or inadvertently declare that their personal preferences should be the standard for other people.

Sometimes these so-called preferences are based on myopic and limited knowledge, narrow vision and little or no exposure to other points of views, cultures and a broad based education. Sure, the Know-It-All may have an advanced degree in some highfalutin academic field, but the world is more than just an academic field. Take for example, a Know-It-All who grew up as an only child in a family of very orderly parents, and now he expects his four kids and wife to keep the house spic-span like he "knew" growing up. The narrow minded obsession with perfection is evident in the desire to attain the perfection he has always "known" even when it can be clearly seen that the circumstances are totally different.

Sometimes the obsession with perfection may come at price. The Know-It-All becomes so afraid of making mistakes that will taint her "perfection" that she is totally immobilized and takes a large amount of time [55] reviewing everything, including useless and trivial details, to be sure they are "perfect" before painfully making a decision; as if the most colossal failures in history were not well researched. Yet when the decision is made, the decision is not effective because the Know-It-All perfectionist may have deviated from the primary objective to chasing an obscure inconsequential side point.

Does this not remind you of people who are so obsessed with details, that they always have their email inbox or physical inbox filled with email or paper details and explanations they requested for whatever they were working on? Of course, they want everything in writing and forwarded to them, no matter how trivial, so they will "know" and then make the "perfect" decision. The part that "kills" you is their total inability to manage the avalanche of information and data that gets dumped on them and so their inbox, both physical and email, are perpetually full and as they toil day in and day out trying to "know" more or rather to "know" everything.

Let us examine another painful and often annoying side to the wishful chase after perfection; general lack of common sense. Just imagine for a moment a corporate manager or director who is a perfectionist Know-It-All boss. He just received a small contract for a fifty-hour project at hundred dollars an hour to create a new five-page website for a total of five thousand dollars. He assigns the project to one member of his five-member team. Each team member costs the company fifty dollars an hour. After a frustrating week of working on the assigned project while the Know-It-All boss trashes the work done as not being good enough, the team member is becomes antsy and fidgety since the Know-It-All boss cannot succinctly pinpoint any concrete problem with the work being trashed. Eventually, the Know-It-All boss decides to hold a team meeting. Two hours later every team member has been reassigned a portion of the project.

Another week passes as the Know-It-All boss repeats the same not-good-enough thrashing exercise with the whole team. He does this of course, with the well worn cliché: "There's got to be a better way," as if real geniuses spend their entire life chasing and sniffing their tails in an endless quest for a "better way." Finally, reluctantly, after a team total of three hundred and twenty hours, the Know-It-All boss agrees the work is "now" good enough. The actual cost of the project to the company is sixteen thousand dollars, not including the Know-It-All boss' time!

Just to perform a sanity check, the first team member assigned to the project at the beginning, deliberately submits to the client her initial creation that was trashed. The client loves it. Then she forwards the "perfect" product endorsed by the boss, and the client still preferred her initial creation. In corporations around the world there are literally tens of thousands of middle managers and directors who squander or fritter away company resources in the manner described above, all in the name of "perfection," as if the most successful companies sell perfect products.

Bully

As we mentioned earlier, the bully we are concerned about in our context are people who use the knowledge they have to verbally or textually or emotionally intimidate others and cause emotional harm or hurt on a continuous basis. For clarity, textual intimidation includes written notes, letters, emails, text messages, chats, forum or profile posts, and profiles. Emotional intimidation may include but is not limited to body language, eye "daggers" and so forth. Some Know-It-Alls that bully, especially in school, often do that to rub in the fact that they are "smarter" while the other students are idiots [19] or to reaffirm their "superiority" outside the classroom setting, perhaps with physical aggression or assault.

In the workplace and social interaction settings Know-It-Alls that bully hide behind textual messages in a conversation and bully their victim. The expression, "hide behind", is appropriate since they write or type things they most likely will never say in face to face conversations. What such Know-It-Alls don't realize or do realize but choose to exploit, is the fact that using electronic and internet mediums causes just as much harm to their victims, if not more, since the victim can read and reread the messages.

Another expression frequently associated with bulling is online abuse which the haltabuse.org defines as "words, gestures and actions which tend to annoy; alarm and abuse (verbally) another person." [56] The misconception that words don't hurt anybody is probably the reason Know-It-Alls tend to bully and harass others online in the name of interactive participation or expressing themselves liberally. Another common misconception that engenders e-bullying and e-harassing is that the messages sent online to other online recipients are anonymous as long as the Know-It-All bully can spoof or use a false online identification. This may be true to a certain extent and for a while, but eventually most e-bullies and e-harassers are caught.

Now let us answer some of the questions posed in chapter 1 which include: What is the most complained about manifestation of all the Know-It-All behaviors? Are people more annoyed with Know-It-Alls who constantly interrupt others to opine their "wisdom" or are people more upset with Know-It-Alls who are incessantly correcting other people like a machine gun stuck in a permanent firing mode? Table 5 below shows clearly, that the relentless corrections voiced by Know-It-Alls are one of the most complained, annoying and denigrating manifestations of all the Know-It-All behaviors. Furthermore, the unrelenting corrections were also more irritating than the interruption of conversations.

Table 5 - Table of Keywords of Some Know-It-All Behavior Manifestations

#	Keywords Searched	Result	#	Keywords Searched	Result
1	"Know-It-All" AND Correcting	23.4 million	9	"Know-It-All" AND Interrupting	0.64 million
2	"Know-It-All" AND Critical	3.17 million	10	"Know-It-All" AND Bullying	0.58 million
3	"Know-It-All" AND Lying	2.46 million	11	"Know-It-All" AND Dominating	0.39 million
4	"Know-It-All" AND Criticism	1.78 million	12	"Know-It-All" AND Condescending	0.22 million
5	"Know-It-All" AND Perfection	1.04 million	13	"Know-It-All" AND Pompous	0.17 million
6	"Know-It-All" AND Manipulation	0.75 million	14	"Know-It-All" AND Assertive	0.16 million
7	"Know-It-All" AND Exaggerating	0.73 million	15	"Know-It-All" AND "Self centered"	0.15 million
8	"Know-It-All" AND Obnoxious	0.69 million			

Source: Google.com search results - 01/07/2011

In this chapter we demystified some of the outward manifestations of the Know-It-All behavior. How do these manifestations of the Know-It-All behavior affect us or make us feel?

Chapter 7: How Know-It-Alls Make Us Feel

Now that we have discussed how Know-It-Alls come across to us or how they manifest the Know-It-All behavior, let us talk about how we feel when they behave that way. The words "us" and "we" as used here are appropriate since the chances are that you too have felt the effect of a Know-It-All's behavior, be it apprehension at their indiscretions or downright humiliation that hurt emotionally for a while or that is still hurting. As we saw earlier, the setting where we meet Know-It-Alls run the gamut, hence from professors who have to deal with Know-It-Alls in class to prekindergarten kids who have to deal with Know-It-Alls on the playground, [1] the chances are we will meet one or have met one or actually live with one. Companies around the world lose large sums of money from the actions, decisions and words of Know-It-Alls on the company's payroll. There are men and women who live with Know-It-Alls that make their life a daily suffocating misery. Clearly, the effects enumerated below don't apply to everyone and may apply in varying degrees and combinations.

Why is it important that we let Know-It-Alls know how we feel? Because it is possible this is the one thing they don't "know" even though they purport to "know" everything. Additionally, we are not whining, and the effect we feel has nothing to do with our level of education or intelligence, after all, a Know-It-All may or may not be more educated or intelligent than we are. Later in this book, how Know-It-Alls can stop or at least curtail the Know-It-All behavior will be expounded and we will also see how we can respectfully "zip" or shut their mouth up without becoming offensive ourselves. So yes, Know-It-Alls make us feel:

Annoyed

Imagine for a moment that you live with a Know-It-All who is obsessed with corrections, and you just returned home from work, exhausted, but trying to explain to the Know-It-All how bad your day was and the Know-It-All kept correcting your grammar, your latitudinal and longitudinal coordinates when things happened, the colors of things you describe and other trivial corrections. Most people will be bothered or irritated or miffed by such a behavior.

There is a time and place for everything. So it is not surprising then that we feel annoyed [2, 3] when a Know-It-All behaves this way because the situation described above is not the appropriate time or setting for making trivial corrections. The annoyance felt could also be attributed to the fact that we feel misunderstood or that we are not worthy of being understood [4] or listened to with respect.

Frustrated

Do you recall the section with a Know-It-All boss obsessed with perfection? Now imagine for a moment that you worked for such boss and toiled for hours only to have your work tossed to the recycle bin with just a cursory glance or a few words, even when there is absolutely nothing wrong with the work done. It could be a frustrating [5, 6] experience would it not? That is why we feel discouraged, disillusioned and dissatisfied when a Know-It-All behaves in a way that thwarts our honest efforts. The honest efforts are not just at work or things we do, but it could include hindering a good conversation with the Know-It-All or with some other person while the Know-It-All interjects incessantly.

Just think of how frustrating it could be living with a Know-It-All who unabashedly tells you they "know" what you are thinking and what you need to do or want to do. Daily conversation in such a household could be full of second guessing by the Know-It-All who is possibly trying to show how "smart" they are at "predicting" your every thought! No, the Know-It-All does not stop there, he or she actually takes those predictions serious and makes decisions based on what they feel you are "actually" trying to think or say, but never quite said it. That is alarming, is it not?

Denigrated

One of the most denigrating [7, 8] circumstances we can find ourselves in is living with or working with or dealing with a Know-It-All hypercritical critic on a daily basis, be they friends, parents, teachers, children, spouses and so on. It is almost like living in a house where an irritating high frequency noise goes off at irregular intervals, making you gnash your teeth in frustration. Or perhaps a better example is an irritatingly loud drip from the bathroom showerhead early in the morning forty minutes before your wake up time.

The negative criticism could actually start from the first words spoken in the morning in some households and continue unabated all day. "There was not enough sugar in the oatmeal this morning, how many times do I have to remind you about that?" "The vegetables at lunch were very peppery are you trying to revive my ulcer or what?" "The dinner rolls were like tombstones, did the microwave breakdown or something?" The puzzling part is that sometimes such denigrating Know-It-All food critics absolutely have no idea how to boil water. Of course, they don't have the manual for boiling water, but they have a wonderful appetite, a taste for good food and "know" all about the act of eating food!

The incessancy of such degrading Know-It-All behavior causes the loss of self esteem [9] over time. It is almost as if the Know-It-All chips away little pieces of self esteem with the daily critic sessions to make us feel less human. [10] In this debased state it is easy to feel powerless [11] and valueless since scarcely nothing we do is valued.

Defensive

Defensive driving is a good analogy to use here in explaining why we feel defensive. A defensive driver observes road conditions and the actions of other drivers and then adjusts his or her driving accordingly to avoid collisions and or injuring pedestrians. In like manner, we have observed the unscrupulous or deceitful ways and under what conditions the Know-It-All gathers knowledge about us and also their actions and usage of such knowledge. We deduce that its use is pejorative in most instances and so when we deal with the unabashed Know-It-All we are on guard against the Know-It-All's hurtful criticism, cutting words, zapping comments, snide remarks, condescending looks, belittling tone of voice and other manifestations of the Know-It-All behavior.

The defensive behavior most often is demonstrated by physically or emotionally establishing a protective barrier [12] between us and the Know-It-All to stop the Know-It-All permanently from hurting us with his or her "knowledge bullets" or at least to curtail or reduce it pejorative impact. A physical barrier may include leaving the immediate vicinity of the Know-It-All or changing jobs by moving to another department or changing the direction of the conversation. An emotional barrier may include mentally tuning out the pejorative words of the Know-It-All behavior and removing ourselves from such a harmful or toxic relationship or friendship.

Ignored

Have you ever sat through an important meeting where a Know-It-All boss or co-worker or friend or relative or spouse or whoever monopolized the entire conversation? It was more or less as if the Know-It-All was a football offense tackle ensuring you never reach or touch the ball, well, in this case so you cannot contribute or add a vital point to the conversation. It is even worse if the Know-It-All is a superior in the workplace or someone you have a lot of respect for, like a spouse or a friend. So, you sit there listening, perhaps glum faced, but totally ignored.

Sometimes, Know-It-Alls might deliberately ignore our opinions, point of views and comments as a condescending way to demonstrate that our opinions and views don't count or that they amount to nothing. Or every so often they will pretend they are listening to what we are saying and then totally ignore [13] our comments and views and supplant it with theirs when the time to make a decision arrives. They probably do this because they already "know" that our point of view is not important and they "know" what is best for us, even when the decision they are making affects us aversely but not them.

Remember that there are spouses who live with Know-It-Alls that not only monopolize the conversation and ignore them but are insensitive to their spouse's emotional well being and emotional necessities. Living in a household where a spouse is determined to subjugate the other by ensuring that they are ignored, don't speak their opinion or point of view can be very suffocating and debilitating.

Tired

How would you feel if you spent a great part of your day defending, verbally and physically, every word you spoke? Or perhaps you spend hours on end arguing about one triviality after the other. Or may be you live with a Know-It-All who loves "details" and so daily they force you to explain in detail the trivial stuff you do for them or present to them. Some conversations with such detail loving Know-It-Alls usually gets bogged down with interrogative requests for details, so much so, that by the time you are done with the conversation you are sweating, your heart is thumping, adrenaline is coursing through your veins and you have no recollection of how the conversation slipped into the danger zone and became so heated. When you regularly live through such a situation at work or at home or with a friend you are bound to get tired.

Moreover, that is precisely why we feel tired around Know-It-Alls who have a preset and unsubstantiated opinion on everything or get a kick out of arguing, even when there is abundant evidence that contradicts their uninformed opinion. Sometimes a headache accompanies that tiredness as we wonder how we got ourselves in this argumentative state with the Know-It-All. Hence, eventually we become anxious [14, 15] or apprehensive at the sight or thought of dealing with the Know-It-All, because among other reasons we find the Know-It-All very tiring.

Intimidated

You probably have heard the nonstop staccato of automatic weapon being fired when the police battle armed bandits or criminal elements. Now imagine that you have a Know-It-All boss who fired question after question at you demanding details or an answer to a question you cannot answer. You cannot answer the question because the Know-It-All boss is actually asking the wrong person and this is the Know-It-All boss' routine and frequent behavior. Additionally, even when you answer or a colleague answers, the answer is almost always not what the Know-It-All boss expected or wanted to hear. Some of us face that routinely at work. In the Know-It-All bosses' quest to show how much they "know" in such heated question and answer sessions they come across as aggressive and intimidating, not just from the tone of voice and body language but also from the sheer force of their personality. It is no surprise then that hordes of employees [17] walk away from their toxic Know-It-All bosses frequently, in companies around the world.

Let us illustrate the issue if intimidation with Webster Know-It-Alls who actually are smart, but have no common sense. Let us further assume that they have an advanced degree in whatever area of endeavor and they are in a conversation with a friend who never went past high school and who is not really into books and all that. You would expect such Know-It-Alls to adjust their vocabulary and thought process without being condescending, right? No, such Know-It-Alls will not. They will try to hold a conversation with their friend as if they were discussing with a colleague in a Jet Propulsion laboratory somewhere in a secret military base in the south pacific. They will use completely inappropriate words, diction, vocabulary and grammar for everyday casual conversation, perhaps to etch in the fact that they have long moved on past the whole high school thing; and in doing so, fail to realize that there are vocabularies for different conversational settings and audiences. Naturally, their friend feels intimidated [16] by the unusual textbook vocabulary being bandied about in a casual café conversation on trivialities.

Besides, we have all met exceptionally bright professors, scientists, astronauts, surgeons, lawyers, engineers, businessmen and so forth. These people hold normal everyday conversations without introducing professional jargon into the conversation; in fact, most people they talk to have no idea who they are. So a Know-It-All intimidating a spouse or a friend or relative or what have you is really a ruse to self promote or show off their verbal prowess.

In the above examples, it is not difficult so see why we would feel intimidated by Know-It-Alls, because they are not being considerate or respectful to us and in reality we are not competing with them nor are we challenging their intelligence or position as Know-It-

Alls. We concede that they "know" everything, even though we don't see any of that in the way they talk and behave.

Dumb

When a Know-It-All friend or relative or spouse constantly squeezes a unsolicited list into your hands, to remind you of trivial stuff or the Know-It-All has sticky notes all over the house to remind you of petty things, even after you have expressed your displeasure over such petty reminders, then, perhaps it is their disrespectful way of trying to make you feel dumb. Or may be it is their way of making you feel as if you are of inferior intelligence or that you totally lack the ability to remember trivial stuff or that you are plain dumb. [18] This is especially true if they have their opinionated justifications to keep up such reminders even after you have asked them to desist and there are no medical reasons for such insistence.

Perhaps the one type of conversation that such Know-It-Alls engage in to make a victim feel like a total moron is when Know-It-Alls condescendingly dismiss the victim's opinions and views as if they were nothing and then gradually restate their baseless and unsubstantiated opinions and actually become indignant when the victim insistently rejects the Know-It-All's opinion. Another type of condescending conversation aimed at making others appear dumb, is a conversation during the presentation of a topic to an audience of peers and superiors. Some Know-It-Alls will deliberately present the material and converse in a way that leaves no doubt that they think the audience is a bunch of dumb people listening to a "brilliant" subject matter expert, even when anybody in that audience could in an impromptu manner make a better presentation.

Clearly, from the above scenarios, it is not difficult to see why we may become upset when Know-It-Alls insistently keep trying to make us look dumb with their calculated and premeditated actions.

Manipulated

For our purposes and as alluded to in the previous chapter, manipulated as used here implies a Know-It-All deliberately using their "knowledge" of the victim's emotions, weaknesses and flaws to maneuver or steer or influence the victim to do their bidding. To get a clearer picture, imagine for a moment that you are staring at someone and without saying a word you mentally will them to get up and go write you a check for a sum of money.

With manipulative Know-It-Alls it is more or less like a mind game or mind tug-of-war going on between the Know-It-All and the victim. Such Know-It-Alls use their "knowledge" to assemble words, body language, select the correct setting and medium and then launch their manipulative [7] attack. This was illustrated in the case of John and Julie described in the last chapter. The frustrating thing for some victims, most often, is the benign and subtle way the attack is launched. This catches the victims off guard, especially if they are resolved to resist the Know-It-All's known wiles, but then the Know-It-All crafts something totally different.

During such manipulative [19] sessions, victims may experience self doubt, question their own motives and intentions and may even feel guilty and obligated to comply with the self serving request of the Know-It-All manipulator. Sometimes innocent people are lured cunningly into the grand scheme of the manipulator, [20] as in the case of a Know-It-All who creates a fake derogatory social network profile page of a victim and then sneakily invites the victim's friends to the said profile page. The actions and the comments of the victim's friends to the victim are part of the results expected by the Know-It-All from the manipulation. The action may include shunning the victim or anger towards the victim, while the comments may be to express shock, surprise or even angry words fired at the victim. In all these scenarios, what has the Know-It-All manipulator achieved? The Know-It-All has deceitfully prevented the manipulated victim from making a personal choice [21], because ordinarily the victim will not behave as indicated, but are now manipulated or maneuvered into such a behavior by the calculating Know-It-All manipulator.

The examples above are just a few in comparison to the manipulative schemes that exist in a Know-It-All's manipulation arsenal and that is why we feel maneuvered, taken, used and annoyed when we are manipulated by a Know-It-All.

Controlled

Even though manipulation is a synonym of the word control, and can also be the direct "fruitage" of manipulation, treating it differently here, allows us to explore the more fundamental connotation of control, that is, dominating or directing someone. Dominating or directing someone conjures up the memory of a puppet being controlled by someone else. Imagine for a moment that the controller is larger than the puppets and so is standing and hovering "over" the puppets like a helicopter.

If we assume that the puppets represent the victims, now imagine that helicopter buzz in a victim's ear everywhere they go and all day. At home, via Commander Know-It-All's voice command the victim is dominated in conversations, told what decisions have been made for he or she given that Commander Know-It-All "knows" what is best for the victim. Furthermore, the victim is argued into the ground literally with unsupported conjectures from Commander Know-It-All's limited or narrow experience in life. Additionally, the victim is cut off in mid sentence as he or she expresses personal views and opinions. Outside the home the victim is tethered to Commander Know-It-All via a cell phone. All phone calls received by the victim also ring at the Commander Know-It-All's headquarters phone, while text messages to the victim will be scanned and parsed later at home to "acquire" knowledge of the victim's whereabouts and text message habits. Of course, thereafter, a decision will be made whether to confiscate the victim's phone or to "restrict" the victim's phone privileges or to "permit" the victim to keep using the phone or some other obsessed control-freak decisions within Commander Know-It-All's imagination. Meanwhile, the victim actually owns and pays for his or her phone plus Commander Know-It-All's phone!

Such Know-It-Alls are not just controlling [22] their victims to acquire knowledge of their whereabouts, as in the scenario above, but they sometimes control their victims in order to outwardly express domination over the victims, that is, to remind them about who is the Commander in charge of the relationship or friendship or association. As we saw in chapter 3 the control mechanism can vary from the situation illustrated in this section to constant and incessant corrections [23] to a contemptuous look or body language meant to control without a word. And so, such a stifling behavior that tries to control us against our will is the reason such Know-It-Alls give us a headache. [22] A big headache!

Shoved off the limelight

Have you ever seen a camera crew in a crowded mall or shopping strip, and the crowd rushing towards the camera crew jostling to be the first to be interviewed on live television? That is the image that comes to mind sometimes when we invite a Know-It-All who likes to shine to a public function or to a gathering of our friends. It is almost as if they switch gears or press some hidden button and transform into a positively phototactic moth attracted to bright light, but in this case to an audience where they can "shine." As part of the positively phototactic transformation, the Know-It-All puts on airs, becomes loud, suddenly becomes argumentative, dismisses other people's personal opinions while imposing his or her own which most often lacks any merit and then the Know-It-All generally dominates the conversation to ensure the strobe light is permanently panned and focused on him or her. Some Know-It-Alls have been known to change their accent to sound different, if such a transformation will garner them admiration or a much needed respect. In such argumentative and embattled state of the Know-It-All, we, who invited the Know-It-All, are completely shoved off the limelight as the Know-It-All tries his or her best to hug the limelight [24] albeit selfishly and to the discomfort or perhaps irritation of everyone around.

If it serves their selfish purpose, some Know-It-Alls will actually resort to using "knowledge" of a victim's personal and private life to fuel their deviant sense of humor, meant to entertain the immediate audience, humiliate the victim and make them popular or keep the "shine" on them. The more the audience laughs and responds to the disparaging humor the more fired they are likely to continue humiliating the victim. In this animated state it is almost as if they have lost all sense of decency and may even resort to revealing a few confidential facts about the victim to see if that will take their few minutes of "fame" to a higher level, perhaps giving them a weird high, who knows.

This shows why we feel uncomfortable and sometimes nervous around such conceited and positively phototactic Know-It-Alls.

Nit-picked out of our wits

Do you recall ever playing with kids or friends or family in an area where there was a lot of gravel and later as you were driving home you felt tiny pebbles lodged in between your feet and the inside sole of your shoe? Although they were irritating you could still drive. That is a typical mental picture conveyed when we deal with Know-It-All nit-pickers or faultfinders all day long. Know-It-All nit-pickers "know" all the irritating and inconsequential or trivial details that are missing from everything we do daily and have appointed themselves the procurators of such trivialities and so they monitor us all day to inject the missing trivialities as sarcastic comments, biting questions, condescending words and nasty stares. "Why are you serving "me" the salad in a blue bowl? Salads are "normally" served in green bowls." "Why is this salad almost at room temperature? It should be a bit cooler than this." "What is the expiration date of the croutons in my salad?" "I think you got a tad too much cheese and cream in this salad." "The bacons are kinda dry, did you microwave the salad or something?" Meanwhile, yes, he is wolfing down the salad and licking his lips! Goodness! Can this Know-It-All faultfinder not keep his mouth shut and enjoy his wife's excellent salad preparation? The funny thing is, he has his eyes closed and jaws grinding away happily even as he nit-picks the salad. It is more or less as if it is beneath this Know-It-All nit-picker to find something positive in the salad his wife prepared. Of course, he is doing his wife a favor by eating the salad, even though his body language says the opposite.

Like tiny pebbles wedged between our feet and the inside sole of our shoes that is how nit-picking [25, 26] comes across to us, very irritating, even though we bear up under it daily. What is most difficult to understand is the fact that we overlook, very readily, the flaws and weaknesses of Know-It-All faultfinders and nit-pickers, while they don't overlook ours.

Bullied

You have probably heard news reports of neighborhoods where a ferocious dog broke lose from its kernel, escaped into the street and unfortunately had attacked a few people including children. While the residents waited behind closed doors, with apprehension, for animal control to arrive and help secure the ferocious dog, no one dared step outside carelessly and no one knew where the dog was, but they knew it was out there somewhere. A lot of bullied victims feel like such apprehensive residents as they go about their daily activities. They know the bully and interact with the bully regularly, but they have no way of predicting if they will be bullied and when.

Some Know-It-All bullies presume that their "superior" mental ability authorizes them to bully, e-bully or e-harass others they feel are "inferior" to them. As we have seen, the medium and setting for bulling run the gamut, and the Know-It-Alls who bully could be obnoxious screaming and cursing workplace Know-It-All bosses or naughty Know-It-All students in a primary school playground.

Regardless of the medium, setting or who is doing the bullying the effect is the same. Like the residents in the above example staring through their window panes, the bullied victims are sometimes helpless and must keep working or schooling for a while before the bully is removed or an alternative work or school is found. Having a Know-It-All bully [27, 28] in the family or at work or at school or in any other setting can wreck emotional havoc in a victim's life. That is the reason we feel very apprehensive once we learn that there is a bully in any location that we frequent regularly, be they physical or online locations, because we don't know when they will turn on us. We also recognize that some Know-It-All bullies are hard to apprehend or catch in the act, because they do put to use their "knowledge" and avoid detection. So until they are caught we must be cautious around such Know-It-All bullies.

Flustered

Do you still remember the very first time you realized your loved one was a hypercritical person or a faultfinder or obsessed with corrections and above all was convinced he or she "knew" everything, including what was good for you and what you "must" do for the relationship to work? Do you still remember the adrenaline rush, the brief mental confusion and the bewildered look that came into our eyes as you stared at your loved one? In this flustered state it sure was difficult to reason with the Know-It-All. If the Know-It-All was the overly assertive and domineering type, possibly all attempts to mend the situation or make peace or calm down or change the subject met with stiff opposition and more aggression from the aggressive Know-It-All. Since such Know-It-Alls often see those peaceful maneuvers and overtures as signs of weakness or proof of capitulation, they tend to stump in and declare victory with even more groundless arguments and other Know-It-All conjectures.

It is not difficult to imagine how we could get flustered [29] under such a flurry of "knowledge bullets" coming from someone who purports they love us but whose words, actions and use of knowledge indicate the opposite. In this disconcerted condition we could become self conscious, [30] especially if the "knowledge" disseminating session by the Know-It-All is taking place in public or in front of our children or friends or neighbors. Just mentally picture the shame [30] that accompanies the self consciousness in such a dress down or affront by a Know-It-All. These are the times we feel flustered and as if we were alienated into the enemy's camp.

Patronized

Have you ever had a Know-It-All roommate or friend or a spouse or co-worker or loved one who would call a meeting, text or call you literally several times during the day to remind you about a meeting? Finally, you arrive at the meeting place, be it in a restaurant, in front of the fireplace, in the living room or wherever, and you are all apprehensive as your mind runs through a lot of bad or negative scenarios as to the reason for the meeting. Eventually, the meeting starts with the Know-It-All deliberately taking his or her time and prolonging the time it takes to get to the real reason for the meeting. Sometimes such Know-It-Alls will fill the time in between with trivial stories and other useless details that only serve to exasperate your already frayed nerves. By the time the Know-It-All mentions the real reason for the meeting, your eyes narrow and you stare at the Know-It-All in disbelief, he or she had called a meeting to ask you any one of the following: "Can you please remember to always turn the bathroom light off after you shower?" "Can you not smack while you are eating with me?" "Can you put your trash can on your side of the office cubicle?" "It bothers me when you move around noisily in "your" bedroom, can you quiet down a little?" "Can you wash your dishes after eating and not leave them in the sink overnight?" And you are possibly asking yourself, why this was not mentioned earlier in a face to face conversation without calling a special meeting.

But that is not all. If someone on the other side of the wall were listening in on the conversation they would think the Know-It-All was talking to a child or trying to "teach" a child a few things they don't "know." Sometimes the condescending tone of the Know-It-All's voice may flip back and forth with hostile stares and glances that betray their innermost anger.

Such a patronizing [31, 32] way of talking to us or "teaching" us what we don't "know" can be very frustrating at times and could leave us speechless since it is difficult to comprehend why the Know-It-All has decided to talk to us condescendingly and patronizingly like a child.

Insulted

From time to time in the workplace some people have the opportunity to prepare presentations on behalf of the team or a boss. The boss then makes changes and presents the material to a bigger audience or to higher management. Have you ever assembled the necessary material and prepared such a presentation, handed or emailed it to your Know-It-All boss who niftily deleted your name and appended his name as the person who prepared the presentation? You probably felt insulted when you saw the "Prepared By: Plagiarizing Know-It-All Boss" appended where your name was when you handed or emailed your presentation to him, and you watched in dismay as he unabashedly made the presentation without a single reference to the work you did in preparing the presentation. When attendees asked questions about things that you already briefed your boss about he would make reference to you in the third person, as if he were talking about someone in a different building all together, meanwhile you are seated right there in front of him. Of course, since he is the Know-It-All boss who "knows" everything, did you expect him to admit there was something he did not "know" that came from you?

Then there is the new company Director with three managers reporting to her and a total of twenty five employees. Eager to "know" everything that everybody is doing she mandates that every employee write a daily report accounting for every fifteen minutes of their time and also make sure their report is reflected in the Time Reporting system. The report, she mandates, should be emailed to her daily. Think about this mandate for a moment. One employee who writes two lines for every fifteen minutes will have roughly sixty four lines at the end of the day. For twenty five employees that is one thousand six hundred lines or roughly forty pages of report daily! That turns out to be two hundred pages for a forty-hour work week. The point is, while there is nothing wrong with writing reports to account for the work day, is it not insulting to the employees and managers to expect them to account for every fifteen minutes of their time in writing? This is especially obvious when we consider the fact that the likelihood of this Director reading a two hundred page weekly report is very scant.

Other workplace rather insulting scenarios include a Know-It-All hiring manager asking a prospective employee to "show" that he or she really needs the job after a long exhaustive interview. "Show me one thing that will make me believe you really want this job." How would you answer a question like that after an exhausting two-hour interview? Stand up and dance for the Know-It-All hiring manager? Change your tone of voice and really grovel for the job? Bribe the Know-It-All hiring manager? Make a conference call to your husband or wife and kids so they can tell the Know-It-All hiring manager how desperately you really need the job?

Standardized tests and puzzles have there place in the employee testing and hiring cycle; they are indispensable. The problem comes when a Know-It-All hiring manager decides, since he or she "knows" all about tests and puzzles, to create his or her own poorly thought-out and non-standardized test and puzzle, and then condescendingly insults you with patronizing words about why your performance means you might not be a fit for his or her team. Meanwhile nobody on his or her team ever took the ludicrous and non-standardized test or puzzle assembled hastily the night before. In case you are wondering what a poorly thought-out puzzle looks like, here is one: "What went up but never came down?" "How can you turn off the light in the next room without entering the room?" And other goofy interview puzzles and quizzes that have absolutely nothing to do with today's Intelligence measures or the job at hand!

In most workplace scenarios we face insulting moments that we ignore or bear because we need that paycheck at the end of the month, but not because we don't recognize the direct and hidden insults lobbed at us frequently.

Embarrassed

Just imagine for a moment that you took a Know-It-All friend of yours who is obsessed with correcting and correctitude to see your wonderful boss who is convalescing after surgery. At the hospital bedside are other friends of your boss, and your boss is in a light mood and a bit talkative. As everybody laughs and banters with your boss, who has a slight speech impediment, your Know-It-All friend, who has never met your boss before, switches into her "corrector" mode and starts "correcting" your boss, especially the pronunciation aspect of the words. You look at your Know-It-All friend and see that "Gotta teach folks how to pronounce words correctly around here" look in her eyes, reinforced with a plastic smile. The word embarrassed does not even begin to address the feeling of chagrin and the cold sweat that envelopes you.

Such embarrassing [33, 34] situations or scenarios are common around Know-It-Alls. This is not surprising since most often the problem stems from not being considerate or not looking out for other people. In other words; total lack of empathy. It could also be that the Know-It-All is focusing on personal "shine" and the obsession to live up to their self appointed position as the vanguard or curator of whatever subject is being discussed. There curatorship most often are based on uncorroborated personal opinions they have on how things should be done or said. This of course, leads to our being embarrassed frequently since we have no idea when and where the curatorial instincts of the Know-It-All will kick in. The emotional harm such embarrassment causes could also be long lasting.

Hindered by ineffective communication

A lot of people have friends or live with Know-It-Alls who will deliberately inject provocative words into a conversation to start an argument or a debate. For such Know-It-Alls they view this type of inappropriate manipulation of others as a way of fostering communication. "I need to get people talking," is the frequently heard punch line from such Know-It-Alls. Oftentimes, such manipulation serves different selfish purposes for Know-It-Alls. Perhaps they want the argument to be a precursor to refusing to do something or to buy something, or it could be a ruse to storm out of the house, or a platform on which to ridicule and humiliate their loved ones, or perhaps the argument could be to impress onlookers who can now see how "bright" they are, and of course, how they "know" everything. In this argumentative mode, Know-It-Alls reject opposing views and opinions and as a result the conversation either grinds to a halt or it becomes the Know-It-All's monopolistic one-sided lecture.

When we are having a conversation with someone and the person becomes argumentative and stops listening [35] it is impossible to communicate effectively with the person, because then you are talking to the famous "brick wall" that is impermeable to words. Excessive arguments and inability to listen to other people's opinions are some of the primary causes of poor and ineffectual communication in marriages, relationships and other social settings where communication is key and vital.

Humiliated

When was the last time you felt the sting of humiliation after a Know-It-All friend or a Know-It-All spouse divulged, in an inappropriate joke, something you told him or her in confidence? As the friends or guests or strangers laughed derisively at you, you perhaps stood awkwardly staring at the unapologetic Know-It-All, asking yourself: Why? For all intents and purposes the only answer you could think of was that the Know-It-All shared the "knowledge" to warm up to the audience, so that he or she may appear very "funny" and "witty." The Know-It-All's desire for admiration and popularity obviously overrode his or her sense of loyalty and decency.

"Humiliation may happen only too easily where idealism plays too prominent a role." [36] Those words of Carl Jung describe appositely one of the fundamental causes of humiliation. [34, 37, 38] Feelings of being dishonored or degraded flourish in environments where the pursuit of the ideal trumps fellow feelings and common sense. In their quest for the ideal, by incessant corrections, acting as if they "know" everything, unabashedly rejecting sound advice or other people's opinions, obsession with perfection, desire to "shine" as the best, most popular and funniest guest and so forth, Know-It-Alls directly or indirectly, wittingly or unwittingly wrest self-esteem and self respect from people around them.

Most of the feelings discussed in this chapter are sometimes accompanied by humiliation especially in scenarios where the Know-It-All behavior is manifested in public or in the presence of other friends or family members or even when the victim is alone with the Know-It-All. For example, in the section on embarrassment the boss was humiliated by the insensitive and inappropriate corrections that drew attention to the boss' speech impediment, whereas the friend who invited the Know-It-All was embarrassed in general and specifically humiliated before the boss. This further demonstrates the fact that in multi person conversations a Know-It-All can affect more than one person profoundly. Thus, it can be said categorically that one of the primary goals [39] of a Know-It-All is to humiliate his or her victim, since the shock effect probably serves to visually and mentally stimulate the euphoria of victory for a Know-It-All. As such, the outward and visible mortification of the victim is probably construed by the Know-It-All as a sign of capitulation.

Without much ado we are most apprehensive of people who have the potential, capacity and audacity to humiliate us in private and in public. Know-It-Alls excel in this regard and that is why we feel humiliated when they catch us off guard or directly affront us with their "knowledge bullets."

In chapter 1 we raised the following questions: How are people most likely to feel in the presence of a Know-It-All; controlled or intimidated? Are people more likely to complain about the humiliation they suffer in the presence of the Know-It-All or the fact that they cannot communicate effectively with the Know-It-All? Table 6 below indicates that one of the most talked about or written about or complained about effects of the Know-It-All behavior is, either being controlled by a Know-It-All, or that the Know-It-All is trying to control the victim. Additionally evident is the indication that the hindering of communication with the Know-It-All is of more concern than say, being ignored or humiliated.

Table 6 - Table of Keywords of Some Effects of the Know-It-All Behavior

#	Keywords Searched	Result	#	Keywords Searched	Result
1	"Know-It-All" AND Control	6.17 million	8	"Know-It-All" AND Frustration	1.31 million
2	"Know-It-All" AND Communication	3.76 million	9	"Know-It-All" AND Bully	1.23 million
3	"Know-It-All" AND Tiring	3.65 million	10	"Know-It-All" AND Defensive	1.07 million
4	"Know-It-All" AND Ignore	2.68 million	11	"Know-It-All" AND Embarrass	0.94 million
5	"Know-It-All" AND Dumb	2.25 million	12	"Know-It-All" AND Manipulation	0.75 million
6	"Know-It-All" AND Annoying	2.23 million	13	"Know-It-All" AND Humiliate	0.74 million
7	"Know-It-All" AND Insult	1.79 million	14	"Know-It-All" AND intimidating	0.42 million

Source: Google.com search results - 01/07/2011

We have declared and expressed clearly how we feel when Know-It-Alls behave badly around us. Why do they behave that way? How can they stop that behavior or least curtail the behavior?

Chapter 8: Why Do Know-It-Alls Behave Like They Do?

Now that we have discussed how we feel when Know-It-Alls manifest the various Know-It-All behaviors, let us find out why they behave that way. We will also discuss the most important thing Know-It-Alls should do. What is it? We will look at ways they can curtail and stop the Know-It-All behavior.

Are you a Know-It-All?

In chapter 3 we defined a Know-It-All as a person who presumes he or she "knows" everything, demands and expects, without merit, to be admired and praised by others for his or her greatness, dismisses other point of views, accumulates public and personal information, and misuses the acquired knowledge with the intent to emotionally injure another person, consciously or inadvertently as well as covertly or as an affront. But, are you a Know-It-All?

Ultimately only you can answer that question based on the above definition of a Know-It-All. However, a self examination, which is usually private and unencumbered when carried out honestly might help you draw the correct conclusions. Additionally, you can ask people around you for an honest opinion. Most probably they will offer an honest opinion. A psychologist or a psychiatrist will be a beneficial source for a firm and precise answer. Nonetheless, self examining questions like the following might help to draw the right conclusion.

When you hear or see something you are knowledgeable about, can you wait and talk about it when it is appropriate or do you have to blurt it right there and then and sidetrack all conversations to what you would like to talk about? Do you recognize the difference between a broadly read person and a broad minded person? The two are not mutually exclusive. Do you receive meaningful contribution from your co-workers, friends and family in conversations or do they just "Yes" along, praise you for your "greatness" and resign themselves to your monopolistic and one-sided lecture? Do you have an irresistible urge to flaunt your knowledge and correct others over trivial issues? Do you get upset when others express their points of views or opinions and they are totally different from yours?

Do you feel the sudden urge to do whatever you can to be the "star" of the occasion even when you have not really contributed or done anything to merit the "stardom" status? Do you feel tempted sometimes to "shine" by using the intimate, private and personal information entrusted to you when having a general conversation with other people? In other words, you use such knowledge to show your audience that you and the victim "go way back" even when that will betray the confidential information entrusted to you. Do you find it hard to accept suggestions or counsel especially when they are clearly beneficial to you but not what you were expecting to hear? Do you feel you have to have the last word or say in any conversation or argument? Do you feel sometimes that you already "know" what people are about to tell you even before they say it? Do you think you "know" everything sometimes or perhaps all the time?

Some reasons why Know-It-Alls behave like they do

In this section, we will look at some of the observable traits deducted by observing the Know-It-All behavior and then analyze those traits based on thoughts and comments from psychologists who have observed similar traits in the past. The analysis will give us insight as to why Know-It-Alls behave the way they do. The attributions, [1] that is, our attempt to explain the cause of the Know-It-All behavior will be primarily dispositional [1] in nature, in other words, we will examine the internalized reasons or motives or attitudes that propel Know-It-Alls to behave the way they do. We will not discuss the situational attributions, [1] that is, extenuating factors or influences that were at play when Know-It-Alls display the Know-It-All behavior. This is appropriate since we don't know what the extenuating circumstances are; besides, Know-It-Alls have a firmer control over their dispositional attributes than they do over their situational attributes. Therefore, they should be in a better position to exert control over the dispositional attributes, some of which are discussed below.

Insensitive

Back in the early to late nineteenth century brick makers used their hand and feet to knead clay as part of the brick making process. It is not difficult to imagine that their hands and feet may have been much calloused and as result less sensitive to the touch. This calloused condition of the hand and feet fittingly illustrates an insensitive person's treatment of other people. Larry May in his article "Insensitivity and moral responsibility" gives a good description of an insensitive person which is cited again here for emphasis. He said: "When it is said that someone is an insensitive person this typically means that that person displays certain attitudes including a lack of awareness of the effects of his or her actions on others and a failure to care about these effects." [2]

Hence, when Know-It-Alls consistently act and behave in a way that demonstrates that they do not care about the effects of their behavior on their victim, we can conclude that they are insensitive. Of course, "one way to be insensitive to another's suffering is to be oblivious to it, but an insensitive person might instead be aware of another's suffering and disregard its moral significance." [3] This total disregard of the moral, emotional and even physical consequences of their insensitivity is one of the reasons that impel Know-It-Alls to keep on manifesting the Know-It-All behavior.

Insecure

The dictionary defines insecure as "subject to fears, doubts, etc.; not self-confident or assured." [4] Other synonyms of insecure include anxious, questioning and insubstantial. In other words, an insecure person who has nothing weighty to contribute in a conversation, for example, may compensate for this inadequacy and self doubt by bubbling forth blustering questions, taking an arrogant or aggressive stance, and perhaps braggadocio to compensate. This is much like a big empty vessel falling to a concrete floor and startling everyone. Let us think about that for a moment. Imagine that we are in a room full of people we assume are really smart, and they are discussing a subject we are clueless about. The natural tendency of an insecure and morally dishonest person will be to put on airs, talk big and loud about nothing and play pretend, whereas a secure morally honest person will see the session as an opportunity to listen and learn.

This compensatory behavior of insecure persons is what Alfred Adler alluded to when he wrote: "A person who is vain and ambitious will inevitably be overly sensitive and insecure as well, and this oversensitivity and insecurity will manifest themselves especially if life does not meet his demands... Obstinacy, faultfinding, and a tendency to deprecate are qualities that grow on the soil of ambition and vanity and express a belligerent mentality in various forms." [5]

A Know-It-All who is determined to maintain his or her reputation as a "go to person" or someone who "knows" everything or to retain their "shine" and popularity will often be insecure. Why? Because in reality no one knows everything there is to know on any subject. Hence, the upkeep of the façade, especially in conversations where he or she cannot contribute meaningfully, or in conversations where his or her contributions are flawed for various reasons and on various levels brings, often forces the Know-It-All to become insecure and compensate by being obstinate, faultfinding, irresponsibly argumentative, disparaging and generally difficult to deal with.

Another surprising revelation related to insecurity is the fact that people in positions of power exhibit insecurity at distinctly higher levels. Commenting on this fact Chen and Fast in their Newsweek article, "The Making of a Toxic Boss" said: "... power and feelings of incompetence interact in creating an intolerable boss. ...people who felt inadequate were abusive only if they also were in positions of power, and powerful people were mean and aggressive only if they suffered from self-doubts." [6] From the foregoing it becomes clear why an insecure and perhaps incompetent Know-It-All boss, for example, will be an abusive bully that screams [7] and shouts at employees.

Narcissistic

As was mentioned in chapter 2 only a psychiatrist or psychologist can certifiably declare a Know-It-All as narcissistic. However, in this section we will apply the definition of the word narcissistic, which actually stems from a Cluster B personality disorder. A narcissistic "individual has exaggerated sense of self-importance and entitlement; is self-centered, arrogant, demanding, exploitive, envious, craves admiration and attention; lacks empathy." [8] This classical psychology definition of a narcissistic person closely overlaps with the broader definition of a Know-It-All and some of the manifestations of the Know-It-All behavior. Hence, it is not surprising that Know-It-Alls are referred to as narcissistic.

A self-centered outlook on life invariably affects the way narcissists or narcissistic Know-It-Alls relate to other people. For example, Feinberg and Tarrant in their book "Why Smart People Do Dumb Things" stated:

"Narcissists are deficient in connection with the world outside of themselves. They interact with other people, of course, but their relationships are faux relationships, because they are one way. ... The narcissist ... may inflate his self-image through achievement that calls attention of others to his prowess. He [or she] will "hit you over the head" with his qualities. ... The impression the narcissist seeks to give is of strength, competence, confidence, superiority." [9]

As noted earlier in the previous chapters the self promotion and the inordinate desire to shine or create an impression are just crutches that help to prop up an inflated self-image. Another source of constant friction in conversations with Know-It-Alls is their rejection of other people's opinions and views no matter the merit behind them. On the other hand they adhere with much insistence and strong convictions to their own opinions, ideas and views even when there is no evidence to substantiate them. It is more or less as if they are averse to logical reasoning. This form of behavior is engendered by narcissism. [10]

One other synonym for narcissistic is self absorbed. Therefore, it is not startling to learn that "self absorbed people... always talk about themselves." [11] You probably have met Know-It-Alls who talk about themselves nonstop. From the moment you run into them until you forcibly extract yourself from their presence, they are bombarding or pounding you with both appropriate and inappropriate "knowledge" they think you are interested in hearing. In a phone conversation with a Know-It-All who talks nonstop about himself or herself; have you ever dropped the phone, stepped away to take care of something, returned and he or she was still blabbing nonstop? This monopolistic one-sided approach to a conversation makes communication with such Know-It-Alls almost impossible.

Poor communication skill

Without doubt Know-It-Alls who are self absorbed or self centered will be poor communicators. Why? As we saw in the previous section, anyone who monopolizes a conversation is likely to alienate his or her listeners. Such a monopolistic behavior is almost a way of telling listeners that their opinions or contributions are unnecessary or not valued. This is true even when the Know-It-All is an expert in the domain of knowledge and the audience a bunch of novices. That is because in the eagerness to monopolize the conversation the Know-It-All may fail to note that the listeners are not listening or following the conversation. The Know-It-All has no feedback from the audience to help him or her tailor the knowledge being dispensed. Hence, the monopolization of conversation raises a communication barrier which makes it difficult to communicate with the Know-It-All.

Such "barriers to effective communication can inhibit the developing and maintaining of intimate relationships. Some of these barriers are failing to really listen to another person, ... being overly concerned with getting your point across without considering the other's views; ... attempting to change others rather than first attempting to understand them." [12] It is not difficult to see why Know-It-Alls who feel that they should be the ones talking, will have a hard time listening. This is because they are preoccupied with the formulation of their own thoughts and what to say next, even when they don't fundamentally understand what is being conversed at the moment. Do you recall ever talking to a Know-It-All who monopolized your conversation for a long time and finally you had the opportunity to contribute and further the conversation? Then, to your astonishment when the Know-It-All started to talk again, they returned right back to the exact point where they had stopped and picked up from there, as if you never uttered a word. Some Know-It-Alls would actually repeat points you just made as if they were stating it for the first time. There is no doubt that poor communication skill is one of the reasons Know-It-Alls come across the way they do.

Low self esteem

Low self esteem is a phrase used frequently in everyday conversation and most often restrictively attributed to timid and shy people; hence the actual meaning of the phrase is not fully comprehended by a lot of people. The development of self esteem emerges when we frequently and consistently compare [13] our ideal ideas about our capabilities or competencies with our actual capabilities in any one or more fields of endeavors, domain or body of knowledge we feel is important. Therefore, when our ideal ideas about our capabilities match or exceed our actual capabilities, we have a high self esteem and if not we have a low self esteem. For example, a highly successful information technology project manager who was never good at programming software might have a low self esteem especially around successful software engineers, programmers and developers. The reverse of that situation is also true. Hence, as we can see, low self esteem can be experienced by people at any level of success if such people feel that their success is in an area they personally don't view as important; directly or relatively.

How does the low self esteem or feelings of inadequacy or inferiority translate into a tyrannical Know-It-All, who holds up the whole morning meeting at work or conversation at home? "The intensified feeling of inferiority is of necessity related to a whipped-up striving for power that can utilize forms of expression and realizations of all kinds. ... All these manifestations, which stem from a low self-assessment, in the final analysis aim at a larger-than-life personality ideal." [14] These manifestations, much of which we listed in chapter 6, are ways in which Know-It-Alls express their low self esteem in a compensatory manner. But much more than compensating for the low self esteem is the need to pretend the low self esteem does not exist at all. Karl Menninger in his book "The Human Mind" words is more succinctly, he said: "Unconscious refutation of inferiority feelings as represented by the "superiority complex" - that is, strenuous effort not so much to compensate for but to deny the very existence of any such feelings [of inferiority]." [15]

This definition helps us to see why Know-It-Alls come across as having a superiority complex, expressed by body language and even verbally. So when they dominate conversations, it is almost as if they are talking [16] themselves out of their nervous state of low self esteem, asserting themselves, if you will. The frequent put downs [17] and the negative attitude [17] that Know-It-Alls sometimes exhibit, are also associated with low self esteem.

Obsessed with perfection

What could actually motivate a person to be obsessed with perfection, especially in other people, that is, have unusually high expectations of other people? Not only do such expectations set up others for failure but they also expose something else. Karen Horney in her book "Self Analysis" pointed out that: "A person ... in the grip of a neurotic perfectionism ... will think that he [or she] is by nature more orderly and accurate than others." [18] That is the problem. The perfectionist Know-It-All's grandiose idea that they are more orderly and more accurate than everyone else, even when there is little or no evidence to support such a claim, often drives them to expect perfection in others. And since "a person obsessed by a need for perfection largely loses his sense of proportion" [18] such Know-It-Alls excessively demand perfection from others or set unattainable standards for others. This is exacerbated if their victim is a subordinate at work or even a child or a spouse in a family or a loved one in a relationship.

The loss of the sense of proportion as mentioned above, was exemplified earlier where a Know-It-All manager makes a team work many hours over and above a project's budgeted hours, possibly with the rational that the extra unbudgeted hours which the company absorbs at a loss, is a justified cost of perfection. This is true, even when past experiences and similar decisions do not support such a justification. What then impels such people to keep seeking perfection even when past experience shows that their decisions or relentless quest for perfection is flawed? It is the same driving factors that characterize Know-It-Alls, that is, a superiority complex and the need to prove they are "correct" and everybody else is wrong. So much so that their feelings of superiority make them decide that their flawed or untested preferences are superior, [19] whereas all they are doing is confuse their individual and personal preference with perfection. This is one of the reasons perfectionist Know-It-Alls insist that things should be done based on how they "know" it should be done, most often from their limited and ineffectual experience.

Inordinate desire to manipulate and control others

Earlier we mentioned that manipulation often is a precursor to controlling someone, in other words, exerting a strong influence on a victim with the intent to direct the victim or make the victim do the manipulator's bidding. The influence may be subtle or an aggressive affront. The bidding may be a mental decision that the manipulator wants the victim to make or it could be a physical action. Thus, one thing is very clear, the manipulator wants to exert a strong influence on how the victim thinks, feels [20] and acts.

Another reason a manipulator might want to manipulate and control may be to "prevent you from making a choice, to feel in control and powerful, to impose their reality on you ... to distort reality, to diminish [or degrade] you." [21] Again, we see the typical manifestations of the Know-It-All behavior including distortion of reality and degrading others as ways to control a victim.

Another way manipulators and controllers control their victim is through countering, [22] where the manipulator or controller deliberately negates the victim's opinions or views constantly with expressions like: "You're wrong." "That's not what you're feeling." "That's not what you meant." [22] Such expressions give the impression that the manipulator can somehow "read" the victim's mind or that the manipulator "knows" what the victim is thinking. Countering as we saw earlier in the book is a tactic some Know-It-Alls use. Consequently, we can say with certainty that Know-It-Alls can be manipulative and controlling, especially as a means to achieve their self promoting and self-centered interests.

How to stop the Know-It-All behavior

Supposing that after you have performed the self examination recommended earlier, and you have read the above section that outlined some of the reasons why Know-It-Alls behave the way they do, and you conclude that you are a Know-It-All as defined earlier, how can you stop the Know-It-All behavior? It is imperative to remember that "intelligence is like your underwear. It is important that you have it, but not necessary that you show it." [23] Let us examine ten simple things you could do to curtail and stop the behavior.

Listen attentively

Listening is critical to good communication and involves paying attention to the person speaking and "really" hearing what they are saying. Hence, listen and pay attention the same way that you would want your listener or audience to listen to you. Make eye contact if it is appropriate. Don't fidget while listening since that creates the impression you are either not listening or itchy to fire back your response. Furthermore, during an intimate conversation is not the time to "multitask" followed by the well worn expression: "Go on, I'm listening" when your body language says the opposite. How can you listen attentively? Most importantly, "repeat portions of the speaker's message to yourself silently. This will help you reinforce ideas and store them in memory. It forces you to think about what the speaker is saying rather than your own agenda." [24] That statement is true. If you truly listen and repeat the key points to yourself, you will tend to remember a whole lot of what the speaker said and you will avoid being focused on what your response will be when you don't have the complete picture.

What more is needed to make you an attentive listener? "The essence of good listening is empathy, which can be achieved only by suspending our preoccupation with ourselves and entering into the experience of the other person." [25] What preoccupations specifically should be suspended? Listen with nothing to prove and don't be preoccupied with your stake [26] in the conversation or get distracted by mentally assembling your response while you are listening. Think about it for a moment. What if the person you are "not" listening to actually states what you are assembling in your head, how would you know unless you were listening? Do not forget the effect or impact of listening with empathy. "A listener's empathy - understanding what we're trying to say and showing it - builds a bond of understanding, linking us to someone who understands and cares and thus confirming that our feelings are recognizable and legitimate." [25]

Without any iota of doubt if you spend time practicing the art of listening and apply the principles stated above, your listeners will listen to you even more and value the knowledge you disseminate to them.

Communicate openly

Communication, especially as it relates to conversations, is the interchange of ideas, point of views, opinions, thoughts, etc. Hence, communication is bi-directional. When you communicate with someone there is more communicated than just the words spoken to convey the ideas or thoughts to the other person. Your facial expressions, body language, and your eyes all communicate what you are actually saying, albeit non-verbally. Hence, if you say for example: "Oh yes, I can help you" but your eyes are hostile and your body is tense from irritation or anger, then you are not communicating your "yes" effectively. Actually it comes across as the opposite. Or, like was mentioned earlier you say: "Go on, I'm listening" when your body language actually says the complete opposite, then you are hindering communication, since the person talking might perceive you as insincere.

Without a doubt then, we can surmise, from the section on poor communication skills considered earlier, that some of the keys to effective communication include listening with empathy as discussed in the last section, formulating our thoughts and response after we have listened to the other party to completion and ensuring that our response reflects a good understanding of what the other party had just said.

Another vital part of communication is not telling others what to do or providing unsolicited advice. "Giving someone unsolicited advice is a communication blunder." [27] Telling someone that the street he or she is looking for is a mile ahead or telling a friend of yours who just got away with shoplifting not to do that again, would not be unsolicited advice because in both cases, although not apparent, a lot is at stake. However, telling your best friend he looks crazy in his jeans and would be better off in slacks is not only unsolicited advice, but your friend may find it offensive; and it may come across as domineering or that your tastes and preferences are always the best. This does not mean you cannot ask your friend if he wants your opinion first, before giving your sincere opinion if he says it is alright to give such. Telling someone what he or she ought to do is a form of unsolicited advice. For example, assuming your friend keeps a large amount of cash in the house under his pillow, you could in a friendly manner suggest and let him decide: "That is a large amount of money to keep under your pillow, have you thought of opening a bank account to deposit the cash?" Or you could tell them outright what they must do: "That is a large amount of money to keep under your pillow; you must open an account immediately to deposit the money. Let me know when you are ready and I will drive you to the bank."

In the following sections we will also discuss other communication barriers to avoid, including domineering conversations, negative criticism and so forth.

Do not dominate conversations

How would you feel if you had a boss in your workplace who totally dominated conversations at team meetings and even during lunch outings? Furthermore, the boss was not just dominating the conversation, but he or she would cut you off rudely whenever you started to express your personal thoughts and dismiss your thoughts while emphasizing his or her point of view. You will be irritated or annoyed will you not? Well, that is how a lot of people feel when you dominate conversations with them and keep cutting them off or interrupting them to stress your opinion.

Do not dominate conversations, strive to have balanced conversations [28] and catch yourself when you suddenly are the star and orator in a communal or group conversation or even with a friend or spouse. In such situations, stop and invite them to share their opinions, views and comments. In a balanced conversation everybody gives their thoughts and then yields the conversation stage, if you will, to the next person. Obviously, some explanations can be long and require a lot of details, for example, narrating a skiing accident, but that does not constitute dominating a conversation. Furthermore, even if your opinion or idea is correct and verifiable; do not push or force your opinion or idea upon those participating in the conversation. The suave and appropriate thing to do is persuade and appeal to the heart of your listeners with logic, reasoning and sound argument. If after you do that, they don't listen to you or accept or adopt your opinion, then let it go. You can always regroup and present your idea differently next time.

Converse but do not lecture, [29] even when nobody minds you hogging the conversation. If nobody is contributing to the conversation, try drawing them out with questions or perhaps, try changing the conversation to a subject that interests them. When you do ask questions, favor open-ended questions such as: "What is your thought on …?" "Can you shed more light on what you said earlier about …?" "Can you explain …?" Good conversationalists never dominate conversations, they make short and to the point comments, rather than long winded comments, in other words they avoid verbosity. [30] This is because long winded comments eventually lead to monopolistic one-sided conversations. Men who dominate conversations not only are disliked but also die young [31] and this most likely applies to women who dominate conversations.

Recognize the signs and control your Know-It-All impulses

Just like the signs of hunger; such as hunger pangs and the signs of tiredness; such as feelings of lethargy, are recognizable, so are the signs that may sometimes lead to a Know-It-All behavior. In other to curtail such behaviors with a view to stopping them completely you must recognize the signs and proactively avert exhibiting the behavior. For example, when someone challenges your opinion or offers a different opinion than yours, what is the first sign you feel? Recognizing that first sign is very vital to controlling your Know-It-All impulses.

There are physical signs [24] which may include tingly armpits, sharp increase in blood pressure, breaking out in a sweat, stomach acid rising, a tightening stomach, sharp increase in heartbeat, clenched fists, panting, feeling of tightness, a headache, trembling lips, inability to visually focus, dry mouth, a shaky voice and so on. The emotional signs may include anger, frustration, apprehension, feeling cornered, feeling hurt, feeling attacked, and mental exhaustion or emotional stress [31] and so forth. The behavioral signs may include a louder pitch as voice is raised, [32] finger pointing, pacing, pounding objects – table, wall, etc., feet stumping, slamming doors or cabinets, smashing or throwing objects, etc.

Unmistakably, there are ample signs that should warn you about the impending switch to become a grammar corrector or conversation dictator who not only dominates the conversation but also dismisses other people's opinion in a snap. Controlling your impulses is the mark of a successfully intelligent [33] person. Why? Because when you have your impulses under control, your listeners will respect and value you more. They will see you as a knowledgeable person who applies his knowledge first to discipline himself. Unfortunately, the reverse is also true. When you let your Know-It-All behavior run wild and dominate you, your listeners will seriously wonder why a knowledgeable person like you cannot apply the knowledge you disseminate, first to yourself.

Accept responsibility

One of the ways to stop the Know-It-All behavior is to accept responsibility for the effects or impact of your Know-It-All behavior on a friend or spouse or loved one or co-workers, etc. Blaming other people for your actions only serves like a weak wooden crutch that eventually cracks and snaps under load. As was stated in the last section, if you don't control your Know-It-All behavior or impulses, people will wonder if you have the discipline to apply the knowledge you claim you possess to yourself. However, when you accept responsibility you show that "successfully intelligent people accept fair blame ... and accept responsibility if it is their fault. They don't make excuses for themselves or try to put the blame on someone else." [34]

Accepting responsibility could encourage the people you have hurt in the past, by your Know-It-All behavior, to suddenly see you differently and perhaps warm up to you and try to make amends with you. They are also more likely to value the knowledge you possess and would be willing to listen and acquire the knowledge you are disseminating.

Stop obsessing over trivial details

If you were reading a 300-page book and you read all the way to page 150 and found out that pages 150 and 151 had been shredded into three hundred pieces, stuffed into an envelope by some crank and placed where pages 150 and 151 should have been, what would you do? Stop and try to arrange the three hundred pieces so it matches what pages 150 and 151 should have looked like on both sides and then tape the pieces together? Or would you abandon the book and stop reading? Or would you kind of guess what was on pages 150 and 151 and just continue reading?

While being detailed or paying attention to details is a good virtue, remember that it also comes at a price. That price can be very steep and unjustifiable sometimes. The price in the example above is the time it will take to correctly assemble the three hundred pieces of the two pages. Let us say that you can assemble it correctly and tape it together, how do you fit the odd shaped page into the book? Of course, you could make photocopies of the taped page, measure the size of the page, cut the photocopied page down to size, buy paper glue, break the book in two, insert the photocopied page, apply glue, and so forth. Do you really think that after going through all those steps that someone else other than you will appreciate the amount of work you invested to fix the missing page? The time invested if converted into monetary terms could it have bought another book with the missing pages intact?

For example, when you are having a conversation with friends or colleagues and you insist on certain details or incessantly keep interrupting to correct grammar and pronunciation, the price could be that they will quietly stop talking in your presence and may over time withdraw from you. Or worse still, when they see you coming they will either stop talking or change the subject to something they feel you can understand without pestering them with questions. Think about it for a moment. If a friend is telling one of his usual tales to ten of you and you are the only one who cannot fill in the missing blanks with whatever you like and instead keep asking the storyteller to fill it in for you, it may not come across like you are thinking; that is, someone who pays attention to details. The storyteller might think you are deliberately showing you Know-It-All. In other words, you are trying to show the group that he does not know what he is talking about or that he is not detailed enough. Hence, learn when to let the missing trivial and useless details go or if you must get the details, be more prudent. You could contact the storyteller later and ask for such details in private.

Furthermore, pressing lists into someone's hands or posting sticky notes all over the house to remind someone of details, especially when it is unsolicited or not appreciated, is a condescending and humiliating way of reminding someone what they ought to do. Why not try having an honest communication with this person and determine the best way they want to be reminded. Remember that "successfully intelligent people ... [do not] obsess over small details ... [but they always] see or deal with the larger picture in the projects [or activities of life] they undertake." [34]

Don't use your knowledge to humiliate and intimidate

No one is in doubt or questioning your intelligence or that you have the knowledge; whether that knowledge is general in nature or expert in nature or knowledge about other people's weaknesses, likes, dislikes and even confidential information. However, if you used that information appropriately you will not humiliate others or make them look dim-witted. Inappropriate use of your knowledge can be very destructive [35] emotionally, because the emotional injury caused can be long lasting and profound. A physical injury might heal quickly over time and with proper treatment, but emotional injuries last a lot longer and leave emotional scars for a lifetime.

Furthermore, remember that what starts benignly as a humiliating verbal affront or harassment can quickly erupt into physical violence. [36] The probability of this happening actually may increase if the humiliating sessions are repeated frequently. Thus, as you dispense your knowledge look directly at the person you are dispensing it to and make sure you are not hurting the person with your words. If you are hurting or denigrating the person, his or her facial expression or body language or eyes will reflect the effect your words and behavior are having on them, even when the person does not say a word to you. Learn to look for those signs and don't be carried away with the thought that you are disseminating life saving knowledge that is solely for your listener's benefit. In reality, the effect might be the complete opposite.

Synonyms of intimidate include bully or frighten. You will agree, that when your knowledge frightens another person, be it in the way you disseminate the knowledge in a condescending manner, or the put down associated with the knowledge and its dissemination, or the fact that the knowledge is directed to other people you feel are less intelligent, then, you are not using that knowledge in an appropriate way. People should be attracted to you because of your knowledge; they should never be frightened away because of it. For example, if people avoid you because your conversations are monopolistic, one-sided, condescending and long drawn out lectures, followed closely by aggressive interrogation sessions that leave your listeners feeling cornered; then, your great knowledge could frighten people away. Moreover, remember that intimidation or bulling, be it e-bullying or regular bulling or e-harassing may include "spreading rumors, making prejudicial comments, using cruel put-downs ... emotionally ... excluding [other people], humiliating, [and] hazing." [37] Additionally, the effect or impact is the same, even if the intimidation is done verbally, textually via electronic devices or online on the internet.

Avoid brutal honesty

Imagine for a moment that you are sitting in one of your favorite cafes with a group of friends and strangers chatting boisterously and all of a sudden one of your friends sitting close to you asks you if you had brushed your teeth? The boisterous conversation hushes and trickles to a stop and all eyes are on you, including people sitting in adjacent tables. Yes! The humiliation is stinging and best imagined. Here is a more indirect but equally humiliating scenario; the friend sitting close to you hands only you a mint and then shifts his chair a little further from you.

What is the problem in these real life scenarios that happen frequently? Without doubt, you had not brushed your teeth. Furthermore, your friend was not lying; unfortunately their brutal honesty was totally inappropriate or uncouth. Why? Probably, everyone on that table having that conversation with you could tell that in your rush to join them you forgot to brush your teeth and they accommodated that little faux pas of yours, and that is the loving thing to do, but your friend perhaps chose that gathering to demonstrate how "observant" and "detailed" they are at detecting other peoples flaws. They could have whispered that in private to you at a more appropriate time. Parents tend to play out this humiliating scenario, with their children on the receiving end, more often than any group of Know-It-Alls.

So, what is the point? When you are brutally honest with people in your everyday interaction with them, most often you only give the impression or confirm that you are very indiscrete in your dealings with others, like the friend in the scenario above. This is because in a conversation or a gathering, it is "a blunder to focus only on what someone did wrong" [38] and to forget or conveniently overlook the myriad of other good things that you could focus on. There is a time and place for counseling and correcting flaws. Frequently, when people are brutally honest to the deliberate humiliation or denigration of another, it is because they lack the self control to wait until the appropriate moment before giving the advice or they derive some kind of satisfaction from seeing the impact of their humiliating brutal honesty or they just want the instant attention of the audience on them for having the audacity to be brutally honest, even when it is to the detriment of another. In any case, none of these reasons warrants making another person suffer emotionally.

The truth about having a reputation for being obnoxiously and brutally honest is that the more you try to prove you are right and an unusually direct person then the more people around you who suffer from such brutal honesty will be determined to prove you wrong. [39]

Discard negative and destructive criticism

In chapter 6 it was mentioned that constructive criticism, when used in a balanced manner and in the appropriate setting, can be very helpful, as it gently and palatably exposes flaws that need to be mended. Negative and destructive criticism on the other hand simply tears down, regardless of how it is administered or the reasons for disseminating it. Supposing your boss at work or your dad gave you an assignment and a list of instructions with which to perform the task. Many laborious hours later, and after you have completed the assignment, he arrives to inspect what you did and immediately blurts out: "Is that all you can do? I thought you could do better than this?" And then, he proceeds to point out a supposedly big flaw in what you had done; although it turns out you had used your initiative for that portion of the work which he had conveniently and glaringly omitted in the list of instructions. Would you feel upbuilt by this interaction with your boss or dad?

If not, then take more time to think through your criticism before you disseminate or administer it. Discard negative and destructive criticism or even an overcritical approach to conversations. It might seem superficially that you are "brainstorming" or "nurturing" or "mentoring" or truthfully "analyzing" and so forth with your harsh and perhaps poorly worded criticism, but it may not come across that way to your victim. Clothe yourself with tact, sweeten your criticism and preface your criticism with genuine compliments, [38] highlight the positive appropriately without being sarcastic or facetious or patronizing or condescending. Criticize positively and fairly by using well thought out thought provoking questions. [29] Remember that criticism can injure a person emotionally [35] and so be judicious in your use of criticism. As humans, we view and accept criticism individually in very different and distinct ways, so don't assume that what works for John will work for Mary. Instead, find out what works for each person and tailor your constructive criticism accordingly.

Avoid or be cognizant of controversial subjects

In every neighborhood, village, town, city, culture and country there are social issues that are controversial. Some of these include but at not limited to sexual aggression, aggression, sexual assault, sexual abuse, date rape, child labor, gender prejudice, racial prejudice, religious prejudice, abortion, animal cruelty, homosexuality, gun control, and death penalty. It is possible that were you were raised or went to school or have visited or vacationed in places where some of these terms are liberally discussed in public without raising any hoopla. Well, now you are in an area where it creates a ballyhoo and so you need to be cognizant of this fact and stay away from such subjects, unless they are introduced into a conversation by consent of all those participating in the conversation. Even then, you have to watch your physical, emotional and behavioral signs to ensure you do not relapse into the Know-It-All behavior. Furthermore, you may be shocked to find out that what might appear to be a taboo in your culture is completely appropriate and acceptable in another culture, in fact, an unbiased person looking at your culture's take on the issue and the opposing point of view can easily see that both are appropriate point of views based on the local circumstances. So, be balanced on your view of such controversial issues.

Keep in mind that in such discussions, it is easy to become or be labeled a Know-It-All if your listeners perceive your dissemination of knowledge on the subject as insensitive. Yes, insensitive to their feelings and emotions, of which you may not be aware, even though you are stating the truth of the matter verbatim. In fact, even if you have very credible "websites" saying exactly what you just said and you showed it to them on your mobile phone; it may not sway their point of views. What is the point? Your audience is completely tuned out, not because you don't have the facts but because you have not taken into consideration their feelings and emotions on the subject. Such emotions and feelings may well be grounded based on bitter personal or group experience in the past. Hence, if you are not willing to take their emotions and feelings into consideration outside of the facts you have, well, it may be best that you avoid such controversial subjects.

Controversial subjects might include subjects which some individuals specifically consider very touchy outside of well known social issues. It could be an incident from their past that they had personally told you that they don't want to talk about or it could be a subject that instantly starts an argument or debate. Staying away from such controversial subjects and respecting the dignity of others on such matters will ensure that you maintain a good relationship with people.

The points discussed in this chapter enumerated scenarios and ways a Know-It-All can curtail, with a view to stopping, the Know-It-All behavior. Evidently, this will take a lot of diligence, practice and patience on the part of the Know-It-All and the victim, but if the Know-It-All perseveres they will definitely overcome the Know-It-All behavior.

Chapter 9: "Know-It-Alls" – How to shut them up respectfully!

Now that we have done our due diligence and enumerated what Know-It-Alls should do to stop their Know-It-All behavior, we have the confidence that they will start by curtailing the behavior and finally stop. But what if they don't stop? Should you condone the Know-It-All behavior especially if it is a source of constant emotional upheaval for you? While the decision and answer is yours to make, it is hoped that your answer is a resounding "No", since condoning such a behavior could lead to physical violence as was alluded to in the previous chapters and or deep emotional injury over the long run.

If your answer was "No" to the last question, then, what should you do since the Know-It-All will not stop? For starters "refuse to let anyone else control what you think and how you feel about things." [1] You will have to take measures to protect yourself from the Know-It-All who is causing the emotional turmoil. Some measures that you can take have been gleaned from the work of psychologists and experts who have practical suggestions for the various measures that are enumerated below.

The expression "shut them up" in the title of this chapter in no way suggests a fierce verbal sparring or exchange where rude and ineffective words are swapped back and forth with the Know-It-All. In fact, the expression "shut up" also means "to stop talking; become silent or to stop (someone) from talking; silence." [2] Hence, you could stop talking or become silent in other to shut up the Know-It-All, or you could take measures that impel the Know-It-All to stop talking or be silent. The word shut also conveys the meaning of "to bar; exclude" in other words, you could mentally and physically bar or exclude the victim from your mental space and life, effectively shutting up the Know-It-All. For example, you could bar the email of a Know-It-All by reporting them to their Internet Service Provider or to the appropriate authorities in your workplace. You could also bar the email of a Know-It-All by simply filtering your email automatically and directing the Know-It-All's email to your Trash or Delete folder. Mentally you could also exclude the Know-It-All by emotionally and mentally tuning them off whenever they start their denigrating antics and wiles. However, the measures or suggestions outlined later in this chapter provide more specific details for handling the Know-It-All.

Recall that the knowledge cycle of Know-It-Alls includes knowledge acquisition, selecting the medium of dissemination, choosing a setting, discerning the appropriate audience and finally disseminating their pejorative knowledge like a "knowledge bullet". If you carefully examine every component of the cycle, it is obvious that no one can stop the Know-It-All from acquiring knowledge, selecting a medium through which to disseminate the knowledge, choosing a setting where they will disseminate the pejorative knowledge, discerning the appropriate audience of one or more people and finally performing the actual dissemination. This is because all those components are within the discretion and control of the Know-It-All. Nevertheless, there is one component or part component that is totally outside the control of the Know-It-All; it is the audience. You do not have to be part of that audience, in fact, if you remove the audience the Know-It-All is totally incapacitated because there is nobody to disseminate the knowledge to or to exhibit the Know-It-All behavior and so the knowledge cycle is broken.

Therefore, refusing to be part of the audience of a Know-It-All's wiles and denigrating put downs is the key method of shutting them up or keeping them silent. The measures or suggestions summarized below will help you ensure you do not form part of the Know-It-All's audience. Since people see and expect various outcomes when talking with a Know-It-All, many measures are enumerated; hence you will have to select one approach that works for each Know-It-All who is making your life difficult at the moment. It is possible that a combination of the suggestions will be required to achieve the desired results. Additionally, choose one or more measures that match your personality, your approach to solving social issues and your outlook to life, since one size or suggestion does not fit all. Note that the suggestions discussed here apply, regardless of the type of Know-It-All or the Know-It-All's domain of knowledge.

Be verbally firm and direct

Do you remember friends or roommates or co-workers or relatives who always helped themselves to an expensive personal effect of yours, thinking it was for communal usage, until you finally confronted them and told them it was for your own personal use only? The peaceful confrontation became necessary when it was obvious they did not understand your frown, the removal from its normal location and negative body language whenever they partook of your expensive personal effect, for example, your brand name perfume. Of course they could all afford to buy theirs but chose not to. After the explanation, not only did they cease and desist, but they kept apologizing thereafter, to your surprise, because you thought they were deliberately taking advantage of you. Well, they were taking advantage of you, the problem was; they mistook your silence for consent to their behavior of cadging off you.

Sure, Know-It-Alls claim to "know" everything, but that is not true, there are things they don't know and that includes how you "truly" feel. Like the people helping themselves to your expensive personal effect in the example above, Know-It-Alls are helping themselves to your expensive personal happiness. It is possible that you have tried communicating with your eyes, a frown, your body language and even verbal cues, but unfortunately the Know-It-All in question did not get or does not understand your non-verbal cues. Often Know-It-Alls are not adept at reading, seeking or interpreting body language or non-verbal cues. You literally have to spell it out loud and clear, in other words, you have to be very direct and blunt, [3] respectfully of course.

State the problem clearly and succinctly, and then firmly say you want the Know-It-All to stop the specific Know-It-All behavior or behaviors that hurt you. Talk about the specific words that hurt you or the feelings the words conveyed that made you feel hurt and angry. Moreover, talk "in a depersonalized way [that is, don't take things personal] ... talk about their actions or words, NOT about [him or her]." [4] Talking about the person instead of their actions might make it sound like a personal affront and distract from the message you are trying to convey. In fact, the Know-It-All might become defensive and resume his or her Know-It-All behavior including interrupting you to defend his or her "greatness" that is being assailed at the moment. Talking about the Know-It-All's actions is more impersonal and likely to be more fruitful.

Whatever happens, be very firm and direct as you convey your message. Do not let the Know-It-All distract you from the purpose of your conversation, which is, to lay bare how the Know-It-All is hurting you and that he or she needs to stop immediately. You can direct their attention to the contents of chapter 8 to help see how they can stop the hurtful and denigrating Know-It-All behavior.

A key factor in dealing with a Know-It-All is your self esteem, which is the "disposition to experience oneself as competent to cope with the basic challenges to life and as worthy of happiness." [5] Don't allow the Know-It-All to make you lose your self confidence or self esteem. [6] This is because "very often we let the social climate in which we live determine what we put on our own belief window. We accept the values of the [Know-It-All] - without considering their impact on either our behavior or our feelings of self worth." [7] This is exactly what the Know-It-All expects you to do, that is, to jettison the cherished and personal value system you have or your personalized point of view, and perhaps forcefully under threat or by manipulative cohesion accept the Know-It-All's. Accepting a coerced set of values without any personal conviction will erode your self esteem or self worth over time, adding to your emotional hurt. This is not to say however that if a loved one or a friend is trying to help you see that a vice, for example, shoplifting is bad and that you should stop it, then, he or she is trying to erode your value system. Value system as used here encompasses appropriate personal tastes and choices in life that are your basic human rights.

Self esteem comprises of two core elements, "one is a sense of basic confidence in the face of life's challenges: self-efficacy. The other is a sense of being worthy of happiness: self-respect." [5] Hence it is imperative that you avoid self doubt since unscrupulous Know-It-Alls will prey on such self doubt, and impose themselves and their denigrating approach to life. Muster up courage and boldly approach this conversation with the Know-It-All. You have everything to gain and nothing to lose by being confident and firm with the Know-It-All.

Just like Suzette Elgin said in her book, "The Gentle Art of Verbal Self-Defense at Work" it is crucial that "no matter what else you do, say something that transmits this message: "Don't try that with me - I won't play that game."" [8] Don't prevaricate in your stance against a Know-It-All who is intent on harming you emotionally.

Identify the warning signs and take action

When the cloud on a bright sunny day becomes overcast and the sun slips behind a dark cloud it most often signals a storm approaching. Likewise as you commute back from work and you see all the brake lights of the vehicles in front of you light up and the vehicles begin to slow down, you instinctively recognize the sign and do the same; tap your brakes and begin to slow down. You do this even when you don't see the reason why the other vehicles are slowing down. In the same vein, Know-It-Alls generally exhibit visible body language or signs before they begin to demonstrate the Know-It-All behavior. If you can recognize those signs early enough, you can take actions that will limit or prevent the emotional harm a Know-It-All can cause you.

Naturally there are physical signs that you cannot see, for example, if the Know-It-All's stomach tightens or there is a sharp increase in the Know-It-All's heartbeat, you cannot see those internal physical signs. But, physical signs [9] that you can quickly spot include clenched fists, trembling lips, loss of eye contact, and a non-habitual rapid eye blinking. Emotional signs include anger that is facially expressed. Behavioral signs that are easily detectable include louder pitch as voice is raised, finger pointing, pacing up and down, pounding objects – table, wall, etc., feet stumping, slamming doors or cabinets, smashing and throwing objects.

Some Know-It-Alls also have a verbal attack pattern [8] that they routinely follow before and during the onslaught with "knowledge bullets" that are designed to humiliate and denigrate you. As we discussed in the earlier chapters, these "knowledge bullets" include everyday words and regular grammar that are cleverly disguised to hurt and cause harm. Superficially, it looks as if they are disseminating knowledge and so they are not cursing or shouting. If you pay close attention you will notice a pattern, much the same way a firearm makes the same noise each time it is fired. So much so that other experienced hunters, for example, can tell which firearm their friend is using at a given moment without physically seeing or inspecting the firearm. Similarly, the police can discern the caliber of firearms being fired by armed bandits in an attack and then prepare a response accordingly. Once you have identified the pattern and verbal cues, you have to take action to stop the Know-It-All behavior towards you. The actions you can take include ignoring [8] the invitation to a verbal spar or exchange or starting an argument. If an argument has already started, tell the Know-It-All firmly and directly to stop the behavior as was discussed in the previous section.

Other Know-It-Alls often voice that they are stressed and may show the stress physically. Pay attention to such verbal and visual cues and avoid lead on words or phrases in your comments or speech that may trigger the Know-It-All behavior towards you. There is no doubt that if you pay attention to the signs, be they physical, emotional or behavioral, and take appropriate action, you will be able to nip the Know-It-All behavior in the bud before it starts or squelch it shortly thereafter. You have to be proactive.

Request for the source of information

Do you remember ever having a Know-It-All friend in your circle of friends who always regaled all of you with tales in the break room or in the park or anywhere? This Know-It-All friend sometimes had tales that ranged from strange to bizarre, but since it was just a relaxing time together none of you had ever bothered to verify what he was saying or asked for his source of information. Everybody assumed he "knew" what he was talking about; after all he was a really smart guy. However, one day, a new friend joins the group and starts asking the Know-It-All for the source of his tales. To everyone's surprise the Know-It-All could not defend his tales nor provide a valid source for them. In fact, the new friend was an eyewitness to one of the incidents the Know-It-All had narrated earlier. Her version of what actually happened and backed up with newspaper clippings was drastically different from the haphazard exaggerated version of the Know-It-All that was full of copious lies.

Clearly, in this scenario no one was harmed by the Know-It-All's exaggerations. But just imagine that someone had acted based on such information or that the Know-It-All was the argumentative type that will launch into opinionated debates. When dealing with Know-It-Alls who exaggerate, are prone to lies or are unusually argumentative, "insist that they give you facts to back up their ideas." [10] This usually puts then on the defensive or they may want to end the conversation or the storytelling session.

Requesting for the source of information should be done in a polite manner that does not come across as an affront to the Know-It-All. Why? This is because that is a way of showing respect to the Know-It-All, and secondly, because the Know-It-All may actually have several sources to back his or her tale up. When requesting for the source of information, be very specific about what part of the tale you want backed up with a source. Avoid verbose statements like: "I don't believe that, where did you read that?" But you could ask: "Where did you read that drinking warm water, especially when we have a cold, boosts our immune system?" Being specific also helps the Know-It-All to provide a specific source or sources that answers a specific question. Moreover, do not insist on the source of information for every thing the Know-It-All says as that will interrupt the conversation. Simply pick one or two points and request for the source of information.

Be prepared to read through the source of information when the Know-It-All provides it. You could lose your credibility if you keep requesting for such information but never read them. Additionally, be prepared to be challenged to the content of the source information provided to you. Therefore, in reading the source of information be sure to read the context surrounding the claim made by the Know-It-All to ensure that it is logically in harmony with the Know-It-All's claim. Thank the Know-It-All for the information provided and feel free to discuss the subject further if you wish.

If on the other hand the Know-It-All consistently dismisses the request for a source of information or cannot provide any, then it is up to you to decide if you still want to be part of that audience the Know-It-All regales with tales in his or her story fabrication sessions. If not, you can take your leave to avoid arguments or you can simply change the subject to something that does not require tall tales. These two measures and other measures are further elaborated on in the sections below.

Don't walk into the argument trap

Have you ever met people who had a penchant for starting arguments? It is almost as if everything you told them was kind of thrown into a mental blender, blended rapidly and spat back out as an argument instigator. "Good morning" to such a Know-It-All co-worker at 7:15am in the morning will be acknowledged with "What is good in the morning? Don't start that mess with me this morning." As you stand perplexed, coffee in hand, staring at your Know-It-All co-worker, you explain that you were just being polite, to which the Know-It-All co-worker retorts: "It is not the good morning, it is the way you said it. It did not sound like a real good morning. I know you and I know when it is real. That's your sneaky way of sniggering at me for being here late last night and coming in real early this morning. Why are you not working late with me and the others?" Of course, your Know-It-All "knows" what you are thinking and can also "read" minds. Before you realize what is happening, you are, at 7:15am in the morning, in a raging debate, defending your polite morning salutation and explaining why you finished your work on time and left at the company designated closing time, while your Know-It-All co-worker who instant messaged all day yesterday and had to work late into the night and early this morning.

It is only when you traipse back to your office desk with your now cold cup of coffee in hand that you comprehend that, one more time, you had walked in the Know-It-All co-worker's argument trap. Typically, they will be baseless arguments, but fomented to put you down or dress you down or make you pay bitterly for something that they perceive you did or perhaps to remind you of who "really" should be the smarter and faster and brighter person. The verbal cue in this situation was when your salutation was challenged. That was suspect, since globally people acknowledge salutation first before expressing any grievance. It could also have been any other verbal cue, for example a Know-It-All who is about to start argument with a spouse could habitually start such arguments with: "Why do we have to eat tuna every night?" It could well be beans instead of tuna for the next argumentation session.

The key to handling these types of Know-It-Alls, who tend to be domineering and argumentative, is to watch out for their verbal cue and once you spot it, bring the conversation [11] to an end and quietly take your leave or ignore [8] the argument trap and change the subject or apply any of the other measures that are enumerated in this chapter.

Use humor effectively

A good sense of humor or a disposition to see things from the lighter and funny side of life, can serve to diffuse a Know-It-All's attempt to impact your emotional well being negatively. That diffusion is an effective way to shut off the vitriolic "knowledge bullets" and "knowledge pellets" Know-It-Alls churn out. This is because "the redemptive power of humor is clear. ... [It] allows people to be "together," restoring relationships that are in jeopardy." [12] Really, when a close friend or co-worker or a loved one is a Know-It-All you have to deal with on a daily basis, especially in a relationship that is getting more sour by the day, then the relationship is really in jeopardy or in peril of floundering and so requires some redemptive action on your part. Hence, if humor is your forte use it to your advantage. Humor does have its way of lightening up even the darkest moments and situations; bringing back cheer to the heart.

Supposing the Know-It-All is obsessed with making humiliating corrections in front of others both in public and in private, you could make light of the situation in such a way that nullifies the potency of the attack or humiliation. In fact, humor could be used to point out the imprudence of the Know-It-All's behavior and present it in the court of public opinion, so the audience can judge for themselves who is actually behaving shoddily. Thus, to a word pronunciation correction or grammatical correction, you could smile [3] and thank the Know-It-All and then turn and tell the audience or listeners, that the Know-It-All is trying to help you register back in a second grade class so you can start your spelling and pronunciation classes all over again. Anything along those lines will suffice to drive your point home to the Know-It-All.

The same principle can be applied to a domineering, manipulative and controlling Know-It-All who "knows" where you are at all times since he or she knows everything, but still pesters you nonstop to find out where you. Those are the type of Know-It-Alls who will look at you and bark: "I know what you have been up to all day. Don't you ever think you can fool me! Ok. You married a smart husband, not a dummy like your last boyfriend." Then thirty minutes later they will sheepishly ask: "Where were you all day? I tried to reach you but could not." For such Know-It-Alls, one day use your cell phone video and record your activities for as long as the camera has capacity and then email it to the Know-It-All so they "know" where you are and what you did up to that minute. Repeat that all day long and when you catch up with the Know-It-All hand over the last video recording so they can confirm that your day was accounted for. Finally, ask him or her if the personalized video tracker you created, meets his or her need to know your daily movements by the minute. Hopefully, this might help the Know-It-All see the futility of his or her controlling behavior. The only caveat here is to analyze first and make sure this particular joke does not back fire by infuriating the Know-It-All even further. This is because Know-It-Alls who are domineering, manipulative and controlling tend to be very difficult to deal with. So, think through this before you try it.

For faultfinders, a comical approach that sometimes works is approaching the faultfinding Know-It-All after the assigned task and asking him or her to help you identify "all" the faults so you can start fixing them immediately. The irony most often is not lost on such Know-It-Alls and they usually will back off with time.

If you lived in a house with someone who humiliates you constantly with sticky notes meant to condescendingly tell you how dumb you are or that you cannot remember basic daily tasks then you may want to try something similar to the following. Why don't you buy a bunch of sticky notes and one day when the condescending Know-It-All is gone, write sticky notes to yourself for every task you do in the house and place it all over the house, make sure to include: "Watch TV." "Drink water when you are thirsty." "Keep refrigerator door closed." "Keep front door closed." "Sleep when it is bed time." "Breathe with your nose not your ear." "Turn faucet off after washing hand." "Walk while inside the house, don't run." "Don't throw hard metal objects at the glass window." These and other mundane tasks that are bound to make the Know-It-All chuckle could be a truly redemptive humor. For a Know-It-All who presses unsolicited lists into your hand for trivial errands, you may try writing a list of all your daily activities from sun up to sun down and then give it to the Know-It-All and ask them to help you fill out what items they feel are missing from your list. Tell them you were planning to follow the final list they approve for your daily tasks. Again, hopefully the humor entailed will make the Know-It-All reconsider their behavior.

The point is that humor if used correctly can get to the heart of a Know-It-All and make them stop hurting you.

Remind them that they are human

Know-It-Alls who are perfectionists and faultfinders tend to focus so much on the flaw of other people that they forget they are human. Most often these Know-It-Alls have fundamental character flaws or lack abilities in areas in which there victims excel. The amazing thing is that the victims often are not in the least bothered by the Know-It-All's nerve grating character flaws. Nonetheless, we saw in the previous chapters that one of the reasons for Know-It-Alls' sanctimonious sense of perfection or snooty faultfinding is because of a self declared sense of superiority.

The reality is that the demand for perfection and faultlessness has no place in any relationship. Writing about this fact, Carl Jung in his book "The Undiscovered Self" said:

> "A human relationship is not based on differentiation and perfection, for these only emphasize the differences ...it is based ...on imperfection, on what is ... in need of support. The perfect has no need of the other, but [the imperfect] has, for it seeks support and does not confront its partners with anything that might force him [or her] into an inferior position and even humiliate him [or her]." [13]

Therefore, when Know-It-Alls who are perfectionists and faultfinders confront others with their flaws and faults, often their ultimate goal is to humiliate their victims, assert their superiority as someone who "knows" more than their victim or indeed everything and remind their victims, albeit indirectly, of their weakness.

One way to shut up or make Know-It-Alls who are perfectionists and faultfinders to stop is by having a face to face conversation with them. In such a conversation and while looking at them eyeball to eyeball [14] for maximum effect and impact, remind them that they too are human. Remind them in this face to face conversation that you never expect perfection from them, nor do you spend time looking for flaws in their daily interactions with you and things they do for you. Tell them that you will appreciate it if they can stop expecting perfection from you and stop looking for faults because there will always be faults in what they or you do and neither of you can do anything perfectly. Unfortunately, this reminder will be necessary from time to time when they relapse into their perfectionist and faultfinding elements with the passage of time.

Propose alternative ideas

Have you ever started a new job or joined a new group of friends or moved to a new neighborhood, and even though your new acquaintances are all happy to see you, and chat with you peacefully there is always that one contentious or querulous person whose body language or even verbal insinuations make it clear you are not welcome? It usually does not take long to identify the contentious fellow as the incumbent Know-It-All of the workplace, circle of friends or of the neighborhood. Of course, they don't "know" you, so you are a "bad" person and they have appointed themselves as the vanguard dedicated to protecting the rest of the group or neighborhood from your "bad" self and other self aggrandizing illusions peculiar to Know-It-Alls.

With each passing conversation the Know-It-All becomes more and more bold in countering everything you say or do, especially if it is not in agreement or in harmony with what he or she thinks is "best" for the group or neighborhood. And this happens even when you are hundred percent correct and you have evidence to back up what you said or did. Already, you can count instances where the Know-It-All deliberately sabotaged your efforts by providing incomplete or vague information and then pretending it was all that was available, and you overheard the Know-It-All telling malicious lies about you as he or she tries to alienate and isolate you.

How can you peacefully silence or shut up this maligning Know-It-All without rocking the boat, if you will? Any of the measures discussed in this chapter may help, however, some people how found it more practical to reduce the direct head to head conflict by figuring out ways to propose alternative ideas that the Know-It-All may not view as a treat to their "superior" status. Why? "You won't change a difficult person by being difficult." [15] That is the key point. One of you has to yield and one way to yield is to "present your views indirectly" [16] and in so doing take the edge of the perceived notion the Know-It-All has, that you are challenging their "superiority" and trying to show you are as "smart" as they are.

Why is this approach of proposing alternative [17] ideas workable or practical? Brinkman and Kirschner in their book "Dealing with people you can't stand: how to bring out the best in people at their worst" stated that "by letting the Know-It-All know that you recognize an expert and are willing to learn from one, you become less of a threat. ...Consequently, more of your ideas and information will get heard with much less effort on your part and less resistance on theirs." [16] In other words, it reduces conflicts and really calms the Know-It-All's feelings of insecurity as was discussed earlier. Experience also shows that with time, if the Know-It-All is just putting on airs and actually knows nothing, before long it will be evident, but first you have to yield by peacefully proposing alternative ideas and this is because "when two people are in conflict about something important, unless each is able to at least acknowledge the other's point of view, the result is likely to be an emotional cutoff" [18] or even an emotional standoff.

Introduce subjects outside their domain of knowledge

From time to time we run into persons who are really experts in one domain of knowledge, for example sports. Their expertise is not just in sport in general but a specific sport, say basketball or baseball or swimming and so forth. It does not matter what time of the day or where you run into them, they talk about that specific sport. If you run into such a Know-It-All in the morning as you walk towards your car on your way to work, he will corner you and update you with the scores, fouls, plays, boos and what have you from the games played the previous night. Walking away towards your car will not save you. He will walk alongside you, briefing you as you walk and then as you enter your car and roll down the windows to say good bye, he will lean on the open window, seen as an invitation, and continue. Later in the day when you run into him at the neighborhood grocery store, he will coral you towards the sports paraphernalia section and regale you with more updates on the sport.

The interesting aspect about such Know-It-Alls is that they are actually experts in that domain of knowledge, but the intriguing thing about them is the penchant for long winded monopolistic lectures that totally suffocates their listeners. Furthermore, it does not matter what body language cues you use, be it yawning, stretching, shifting around in your seat, shifting your weight from one leg to the other, wiggling your toes, clearing your throat as if you wanted to say something, checking your text messages, checking emails on your cell phone and you name it, it does not work. Your only savior might be a phone call to which you likely would have to spontaneously jump up and literally run away to answer. Those are the types of Know-It-Alls who keep talking on a phone call until you finally fall asleep and wake up minutes later and they are still talking!

One effective way to ensure such Know-It-Alls don't even start their harangue is by beating them to the punch and introducing a subject from a different domain before they get started. Use questions to draw them out and keep them talking on the new subject. Naturally, such a Know-It-All might feel out of his element and awkward, but that also serves to prevent an unusually prolonged one-sided conversation. Hopefully, by the time the Know-It-All works his way back to his favorite domain and starts to drone, you will be long gone.

In today's electronic age there are other ways you can handle such Know-It-Alls especially if you have to deal with them on a regular or daily bases. Just before you start your visit, simply set the alarm on your cell phone to whatever time you want to escape from the Know-It-All. Next, set the ring tone for the alarm to match that of a cell phone call. Once your alarm goes off, jump up and escape! As you leave, tell the Know-It-All you have to go and you don't have to explain if it is a call or not, after all, they are not entitled to that information.

Reject negative criticism

Normally, constructive criticism contains acknowledgement of something positive, be it just the effort invested by the person being critiqued or simply kudos for parts of a job well done. Next, the critic outlines to the person being critiqued what needs to be done to improve or enhance or fix or move to the next stage. The effect most often is mutually upbuilding.

Negative criticism on the other hand is "making a negative evaluation of the other person, her [or his] actions, or attitudes." [19] Often, its premeditated or inadvertent target is you and its motive or purpose is to tear down or destroy, denigrate and humiliate. This is especially true when there is no merit to the criticism or the expressions the criticism embodies.

When you first receive the criticism, constructive or negative, evaluate the criticism and search for things you could work on, or flaws being highlighted that you can improve on. After you identify things that you can improve upon, start by thanking the Know-It-All who is criticizing you, honestly acknowledge that you appreciate them bringing to your attention things that you need to work on, and then enumerate what they are. You can elucidate how you intend to work on what you just enumerated, and if it is appropriate, give timelines and other facts that will indicate your preparedness and seriousness about fixing the flaws identified. Use the Know-It-All's personal first and last names while addressing him or her [20] if this is appropriate in the circumstances. Doing this provides a prima facie evidence that you accepted the criticism in good fate and are ready to apply it. If there are negative elements mixed with the positive in the criticism, it is best to ignore the negative and focus on just the positive and in so doing shut the Know-It-All critic up, since your acceptance of the positive is for your own good.

However, "it is instinctive for people to focus on the negative instead of the positive ... to criticize, to focus on flaws and denigrate new ideas" [21] hence occasionally we meet Know-It-Alls who use negative criticism to denigrate, control and gain an upper hand over their victim. In such cases, there usually is nothing positive in the criticism and the criticism often is an attack against your person and not on anything you have done. The attack might include outright lies, slander, malicious insinuations and pretentious outrage. Sometimes, Know-It-Alls use this for the purpose of proving themselves "right" while they discredit you, or they may use it as a tool to prove that you don't know as much as they "know." In the face of such negative criticism by a Know-It-All who is out to protect his Know-It-All tuff, you can apply some of the other measures outlined in this chapter. Nevertheless, if it is appropriate, especially in the case of slander or malicious lies, you could, on the spot, unequivocally rebuff the falsehood and negative criticism. Specifically and clearly outline the falsehood to the Know-It-All and all in the audience who heard the Know-It-All's malicious slander and negative criticism. Tell the Know-It-All that you do not appreciate their negative criticism and sheer lies told to assassinate your character. Being firm with the Know-It-All might deter them from offering negative criticism meant to tear down in the future.

Use questions and comments effectively

How do you react when people ask you questions that are completely different from what you were thinking about at that point in time or a question that requires or evokes answers different from the one you just gave? Is it not true that it sets your thinking process in motion, as you mull over the question, formulate your answer and then respond to the question? The change from one thought process to the other in order to answer the questions, perhaps, prevented a conversation that was centered on one subject. Additionally, the questions allowed others to participate in the conversation, and the chances are that your answers will be pointed and very specific to the questions asked. Furthermore, the possibility of lecturing is drastically reduced since the questions broke up the conversation into manageable chunks, if you will.

The effective use of questions and comments changes the gears of a conversation from a one-way monopolistic lecture, to a conversation in which participants are not just telling but actively participating by asking [22] questions. This technique can be used to break the vice like grip that Know-It-Alls have when they monopolize conversations and lecture everybody about all that they "know" on a particular subject. It is also a powerful tool when dealing with a Know-It-All who exaggerates a lot. It can be used for virtually any of the Know-It-All behaviors to draw out what actually is going on in the mind of the Know-It-All other than the pre-canned "knowledge" he or she is disseminating at the point in time. The use of questions forces the Know-It-All to be more specific in his or her response.

Tactfully using questions to elicit comments additionally allows you to contribute in a depersonalized way, in other words, the Know-It-All does not feel affronted or challenged. Use well thought out questions to keep the conversation beneficial to you and other participants. If the other participants follow your lead and ask pointed questions, the chances are the Know-It-All will be forced to answer the questions introduced by a participant instead of chasing after their own agenda. When asking questions, favor using who, what, when and why questions, [23] as these types of questions streamline the conversation and keep arguments at bay. Weigh your words carefully, rephrase the question in a more appropriate way if necessary and think through your answers before you utter them, this ensures that the conversation does not deteriorate into an argumentation session.

Susan Benjamin's book "Perfect Phrases for Dealing with Difficult People" enumerates seven key factors for communicating with difficult people. This includes being objective and using examples of instances when the Know-It-All hurt you verbally. [24] This principle can also be applied when formulating questions you want to ask the Know-It-All in a conversation about his or her behavior or actions towards you. State what happened specifically and then follow that with the intended question about the incident.

Questions can be used as a powerful tool to make people begin to think in a different direction, perhaps asking a Know-It-All well thought out questions might evoke deeper thoughts about his or her Know-It-All behavior and lead to change.

Be assertive and convincing

Scientists tell us that sharks can smell a drop of blood from a quarter [25] of a mile away or in a million drops of water at sea. This minuscule drop of blood in comparison to the millions of drops generally signals to the shark that there is a prey in distress. In other words, the shark has detected a sign of weakness in a prey. Often, some species of sharks follow the scent of the drop of blood and make a meal out of the prey especially if it is an animal in their food web.

Similarly, Know-It-Alls who are domineering and overbearing can quickly identify a weak victim during their conversational knowledge dissemination sessions and take advantage of that weakness to control and direct the victim's life. You probably have seen or heard of men or women who are domineering and overbearing Know-It-Alls that are married to victims whom they dominate and crush daily with their Know-It-All behavior. Think about it for a moment; is it not true that when you see someone who is unsure of themselves, shifty, cannot make eye contact, tends to ramble when they talk, lacks poise and generally lacks confidence, it is a bit difficult to take them serious? Now, imagine such a person, feebly trying to communicate to a domineering and overbearing Know-It-All to stop his Know-It-All behavior. He or she will not be very convincing, right?

It is true that the word assertive also means domineering or confident, but the context as used in this section will be to display confidence convincingly. But, what really is assertiveness? "Assertiveness is about letting others know what you do [want] and do not want in a confident and direct way ... this means calmly stating your needs, what you will or will not accept, and how you want to be treated." [26] The challenge here is that the Know-It-All may have hurt you for such a long time emotionally that he or she probably thinks this is alright with you since you have never convincingly stated that you do not want to be talked to or treated that way. It is imperative then, that you talk in a confident and convincing way to the Know-It-All. This might mean calling a special meeting or changing the venue where you had talked to them in the past or carefully choosing a different set of words to strongly convey your desires as to how you want to be treated.

Why should you be assertive or demonstrate confidence in a convincing way? "Assertion skills [are] verbal and nonverbal behaviors [that] enable you to maintain respect, satisfy your needs, and defend your rights without dominating, manipulating, abusing or controlling others." [27] That is precisely what you want to do; defend your basic human rights to live peacefully without someone cutting you down on a regular bases with "knowledge bullets" that are sometimes well disguised but nonetheless fired to disrespect and humiliate you. Furthermore, it helps you retain your self-dignity. Even so, remember that aggression just like passiveness has no place in a friendship, relationship or even marriage. Thus, express your sentiments or irritation verbally and in a non provocative manner. Be sure to ask the Know-It-All verbally and firmly to stop the Know-It-All behavior. Outline unmistakably and concisely the Know-It-All behavior or behaviors that you want them to stop. Do not vacillate in your determination to get your point across assertively. Confidence helps you assert yourself so you can "talk openly with the other [person] about matters of significance to the relationship [or friendship or marriage]. The two persons can openly express grievances and let each other know the changes they desire." [28] This should be your goal. Hopefully your assertively asking the Know-It-All to stop will yield good results.

Listen and do not interrupt

One of the most frequent complaints against Know-It-Alls is that they don't listen to the other person by either cutting them off verbally or cutting them off mentally while preparing a response, or a counterattack, even when the Know-It-All has not listened to the other person's comment. Some Know-It-Alls will actually ignore your comment and continue their point where they stopped before you interrupted them. Either way, such behavior can be very frustrating to a victim trying to communicate a genuine and important point. However, like we said at the beginning of this chapter, if there is no audience, the Know-It-All will not display the Know-It-All behavior and there will be no arguments or humiliating put downs. Therefore, one way to keep the Know-It-All silent, so to say, is by listening attentively and not interrupting. This way, an argument will not erupt and you can choose another time, a better and more appropriate setting to respond to the Know-It-All.

Listening attentively without interrupting or making any comment takes the pressure off the Know-It-All. He or she might curtail or scale back on the Know-It-All behavior if they don't feel the pressure to "act" as a Know-It-All. Listening attentively calls for being an empathetic listener, which is one of the fundamentals of being a good listener. [18] You can show that you are an empathetic listener from your body language and facial expressions while listening to the Know-It-All. This does not mean you agree to what the Know-It-All is saying or that you condone the Know-It-All's obnoxious behavior. This is simply a strategy to maintain peace and prevent a futile argument that incessantly plagues your friendship or relationship or marriage. It is also important that you listen with nothing to prove and don't be preoccupied with your stake [29] in the conversation.

This idea or strategy of listening without interruption and saving your response for another time is quite pervasive. If you recall, you probably have been in a meeting or gathering and someone, perhaps a Know-It-All said something totally wrong or bizarre, but nobody present corrected him or her on the spot or that very day. Nevertheless, a while later and in a more appropriate setting someone presented a rebuttal that disproved or exposed the Know-It-All's conjectures as a big lie or totally inaccurate. Additionally, listening without interruption and leaving the response for another day allows you to think through what was said and distill the salient points that need to be addressed. This contrasts sharply with giving a seat of the pants response that is not well thought out and only helps to convene a big headache creating argumentation session.

Change the subject

Imagine for a moment that you have young children in your house. One day while you are in the kitchen cooking you hear a big racket going on in your living room. As you approach the living room to inspect, you see your children all acting wildly as they try to imitate the action scene of a very violent movie they are watching on television. What do you think will happen if you pick up the television remote and change the channel? Most likely the commotion will die down. Often people employ this same approach in conversations that are going awry. This can be true in conversations with Know-It-Alls who are extremely argumentative, and will not listen to other opinions, especially in a domain of knowledge where they actually have a wealth of knowledge. Such conversations often turn personal and very negative when the Know-It-All realizes that his or her "expert" opinion is not gaining any traction with the listeners.

As is usual in every conversation, they start like any normal conversation, but then there comes the inflection point in the conversation where the conversation suddenly changes drastically from being positive and upbuilding to a negative, degrading and humiliating conversation. This inflection point is often crossed first by the Know-It-All who may subconsciously relapse into his or her old ways or is simply trying to assert their "superior" point of view or knowledge. If you are watchful you will observe the signs associated with crossing the inflection point. Once you see the signs you may want to pause the current conversation with the Know-It-All by first staring fixedly at him or her for a moment and then quietly changing the subject to something radically different from the current subject of conversation. Why is the fixed stare effective? "The silent, expressionless, blank stare occurs when you immediately stop everything you are doing and freeze as you blankly stare down your opponent. This often throws your verbal adversary so off balance" [30] that when you change the subject they have no choice but follow suit. Furthermore, the stare serves almost like a warning that says: "Don't even start that argumentation session with me."

To understand the impact of changing the subject to something radically different, imagine for example, that you and your spouse are watching a sporting event on television. Gradually the conversation turns to the color of the jerseys worn by the two teams. You and your spouse have different ideas about the appropriate color for each of the teams based on their mascots. Suddenly, in the heat of the conversation, the conversation turns argumentative and your spouse is condescendingly lecturing and firing "knowledge bullets" at you about the significance of the colors you chose and how that reflects and relates to your flaws and weaknesses. In short order, your flaws and weaknesses become the principal focus of the argument. As the argument turns into a bedlam and you are making a defense to preserve what is left of your dignity, your child enters and tells the two of you that the dinner on the stove is on fire and spreading. What do you think will happen to the heated argument? The outcome would be similar to someone puncturing a balloon noisily with a pin or as if someone had poured a bucket of cold water on you and your spouse. Likely two of you will sprint to the kitchen to attend to something more important and together for that matter.

So do not underestimate the power of changing the subject to something radically different and less controversial. If you use this strategy the effect will be like pouring a bucket of ice cold water on your raging argument with a Know-It-All.

Strongly convey your disapproval

Have you observed with your own children or perhaps the children of other people that they respond in different ways to verbal and non-verbal admonitions? For some children, a hard stare, a shaking of the head from side to side, a clap of the hand followed by a frown, standing with arms akimbo followed by a stare and so forth, will get their attention, resulting in their ceasing or desisting to do whatever was the source of consternation. For other children, the aforementioned body language does not cut it; you have to verbally tell them to stop. And yet for other children, both verbal and non-verbal cues do not work and usually a unique solution tailored to such children may be adopted to get them to cease and desist from the bad behavior. This analogy can be applied to Know-It-Alls as well.

Thus far in this chapter we have talked about having a firm heart to heart conversation with the Know-It-All where you lay out respectfully all the Know-It-All behaviors that are causing you grief emotionally. It was also mentioned that some Know-It-Alls, just like some people, are not adept at reading or interpreting body language and non-verbal cues. Nonetheless, there are Know-It-Alls who are adroit at interpreting body language and non-verbal cues. This is to be expected since "only a small percentage of communication involves actual words: 7%, to be exact. In fact, 55% of communication is visual (body language, eye contact) and 38% is vocal (pitch, speed, volume, tone of voice)." [30] Take eye contact for example, it readily helps us access another person's sincerity, albeit imperfectly, but all the same just as useful. Someone's eyes and facial expression may indicate hostility or anger or frustration, while his or her verbal expressions through words are saying something totally different. If we add the voice timbre to the mix it helps us get a good gauge of the person we are communicating with.

This powerful tool, that is, our body language, can be used as a force for good in silencing a Know-It-All not only while they are disseminating their "knowledge bullets" but even much later. This is practical when verbal communication is not possible or could worsen the situation. Indeed, this can be used effectively in situations where the Know-It-All is an acquaintance or a friend or a spouse or a co-worker whom we had invited to accompany us somewhere and on arrival begin to display the Know-It-All behavior. In such situations convey your strong disapproval with a facial expression, lock eyes or use any form of body language that is most effective and make sure your message is received clearly. Lillian Glass in her book "Complete Idiots Guide to - Verbal Self-Defense" described one of such body language strategies saying:

"[In] the look of disgust strategy ... you have an expression of disgust. ...someone [is] scowling at him in disgust, staring at him, and saying nothing." [31] If the Know-It-All "gets" the point, he or she will most likely adjust and curtail the Know-It-All behavior, at least for the time being.

Be patient and understanding

It has been mentioned several times in this book that some Know-It-Alls demonstrate the Know-It-All behavior unwittingly. They don't set off with the intention that they "know" everything or that they want to argue everybody else into the ground so they would be the only ones standing in victory lane as the "correct" debaters. Most often, one thing leads to another and before they know it they are engrossed, hook, line and sinker in the Know-It-All behavior. If you recall in chapter 7 under the section "Shoved off the limelight" we discussed conceited and positively phototactic Know-It-Alls. Such Know-It-Alls tend to be swayed heavily in the midst of a group or crowd of people as well as peers, so much so that they begin to exhibit different mannerisms, including the Know-It-All behavior. The irony is that when you are alone with them they behave differently and rarely display the Know-It-All behavior. In fact, some may apologize for their surreal behavior. There are also many other Know-It-Alls who display different Know-It-All behaviors who are constantly working to curtail such behaviors.

In situations like this, patience and an outward demonstration of understanding and support might help the Know-It-All to keep working to curtail and eventually stop the Know-It-All behavior. Understanding may include staying away or not inviting the Know-It-All to situations that will bring out the behavior, being willing to discuss the problem without being overly judgmental or worried about the embarrassment they caused you the last time, helping them locate professional help if appropriate and providing feedback if any from other people who have observed the Know-It-All behavior. The words of Carl Jung help to put this in perspective. Jung said: "when the individual is willing to fulfill the demands of rigorous self examination and self-knowledge... he [or she] will not only discover some important truths about himself [or herself], but will ... have succeeded in deeming himself [or herself] worthy of serious attention and sympathetic interest." [32] Thus, your patience and understanding could well be the aid the Know-It-All needs to stop the Know-It-All behavior.

Journalize the humiliating conversations

Have you ever wondered why most people steal things when no one is looking or most often cover their face while stealing in public or why some people burn or shred documents to cover evidence or why people tell lies to cover other lies and situations? While there may be many reasons, the one of interest in the context of this section is that naturally humans do not want permanent records made of their bad behavior or faux pas. This repugnance or being averse to having bad behavior recorded also serves as a deterrent. This is the reason most people behave better, relatively, when they know they are being observed.

The idea suggested here in no way endorses electronically recording your conversation with the Know-It-All without their consent or knowledge. Electronically recording your conversation without someone's consent is illegal in a lot of jurisdictions. In fact the idea stated here, if used properly will deter the Know-It-All from his or her Know-It-All behavior and there may be no reason to journalize a whole lot, if at all.

As we have learned from the various chapters of this book some Know-It-Alls use every opportunity to self promote, dismiss other peoples' opinions and could get extremely argumentative even when there is no basis for argument. Still others can launch into abusive and condescending knowledge disseminating sessions that are meant to denigrate and humiliate their victim. A lot of times these scenarios are played out between just the Know-It-All and the victim and could easily escalate to physical violence. One way to bring such a rapidly deteriorating situation under control, especially if the Know-It-All is not prone to violence and is still reasonable, is to grab your diary or journal and pen, then, seated within sight of the Know-It-All tell him that you are writing down in your journal all that he is saying, word for word. Another way to use the journal may be to write the events that happened and the precise expressions and words that cut deep and hurt. When things have calmed down, share the journal with the Know-It-All so he can see and read the "knowledge bullets" he had fired at you during the last argumentation session.

As stated at the onset, most humans naturally do not want their negative behavior to be recorded in writing. Hence, the idea of having the Know-It-All's inappropriate verbiage written down should serve as a deterrent to make him or her desist from the Know-It-All behavior.

Refuse to be rudely interrupted

Have you ever stepped into the front passenger seat of someone's car and it turns out the radio was tuned to a station whose newscasters spoke a language you did not understand or the station was playing music you did not really care for? Since you were the only one in the vehicle, waiting for the driver, were you tempted to reach out and change the station or turn off the radio? Such a reaction is common when a scratched compact disc or CD is stuck playing the same tune or sentence over and over again. This leads to the question: Do people and indeed Know-It-Alls who incessantly interrupt others to fire through their own opinions and views perceive others like broken or scratched CDs that need to be turned off? Furthermore, is it not true that if a Know-It-All is so busy rehearsing her verbal counterattack that it is possible she is not listening or paying attention to what is being said by the other party and so it sounds like a scratched CD?

Regardless of the reason for interrupting others when they are talking, one of the most fundamental rules of verbal exchange [33] or conversation is not to interrupt people when they are talking. Firstly, it shows the person interrupting is not a polite, empathetic and good listener. Secondly, it shows a total lack of respect to the person talking. This is even more evident when the interrupter airs views or opinions which show clearly he or she had not been listening to the other participants of the conversation. This eagerness to interrupt and regain control of the knowledge dissemination session is a tendency common with Know-It-Alls who monopolize conversations, or Know-It-Alls who are excessively argumentative and are determined at all cost to show how "right" they are and how "wrong" everybody else is, or it could be that the Know-It-All sees his audience as completely beneath him and hence will not listen to their views and opinions.

At any rate, do not let the Know-It-All interrupt you while you are talking. State clearly that you allowed the Know-It-All to talk without interrupting him or her. Hence, the Know-It-All should allow you to contribute your point of view without interruption. You can preface your response by reminding the Know-It-All not to interrupt you during your response. Be firm and confident when you make this request, that way the Know-It-All will know you are serious and do exactly as you bid, that is, keep quiet while you marshal out your point. It behooves you to listen to the Know-It-All without interrupting him or her, thus setting a good example.

Do not respond to a bully

In various sections of this book it was mentioned that the medium for bulling can be verbal, electronic or online. In spite of the medium used, the primary purpose of bullying is to intimidate the victim with the sole purpose of humiliating, eliciting angry and hurt feelings. In reality, electronic and online "kind of abuse would rarely occur in person, but because of the [relative] anonymity that the internet [or other electronic devices] provides, many people will take it upon themselves to vent their anger at you in the form of an abusive or harassing email" [34] or text messages or false profiles or vitriolic comments in a forum posting.

Do not respond [35] to the bully verbally, electronically or through internet based mediums. For Know-It-Alls who bully, your response may serve to feed the impetus they have, because they can read your response and sense your anger and hurt feelings. Since such Know-It-Alls often derive joy and pleasure from hurting others, they may want to continue the bullying to elicit more hurt feelings from you or simply to get more kicks out of it. Even in a face to face encounter, a Know-It-All bully may relish your body language feedback that indicates you are angry and hurt.

While silence is the best answer to such Know-It-All bullies, save emails, text messages and every bullying paraphernalia sent to you electronically or through the internet or physically since you may need that to litigate. Furthermore, if the Know-It-All sexually or physically threatens you, then you must report the Know-It-All bully immediately to law enforcement officials in your locality. Why? This is because the person who threatens sexual or physical violence today may indeed carry out such a threat tomorrow.

A more complex scenario arises when the Know-It-All bully is your direct boss or a superior or a co-worker. In either case you can apply any of the measures listed in this chapter first and let the Know-It-All bully know, in a very respectful manner, how his or her Know-It-All behavior makes you feel. This concession to a Know-It-All bully is necessary since this is a workplace and there is a possibility that because everyone else he or she bullies keeps quiet, the Know-It-All bully thinks it is alright to do so to everyone else. If after communicating your feelings to the Know-It-All bully at work, he or she persists with bullying, then, your next step should be reporting the Know-It-All bully to his or her immediate superior.

Although a face to face meeting with the immediate superior is fine, it will be better if you initiate your first contact with a well worded email detailing what the Know-It-All bully had said or done and be sure to copy yourself or keep a copy of the email. It will even be better if you can attach the email or scanned hand written note from the Know-It-All bully with the offensive content if applicable. If the Know-It-All bully's immediate superior is lackadaisical about the bullying or trying to play it down or is trying to make you look like a bad team player and so on, then, it is time to contact a neutral party in your workplace and that most often will be the Human Resource department. Follow your workplace established procedures for filing and reporting grievances. If you don't have a Human Resource department, then, talk to the owner of the business where you work. If the Know-It-All bully is the owner of the business, then, you have to decide the best course of action. If the bullying is affecting your mental well being, then, may be it will be best to look for another employment.

Stay away from controversial subjects

The warmth that comes from a fireplace is invigorating in cold weather. The glowing red hot pieces of coal or charcoal from the burning wood are reassuring as they sit in a heap in the middle of the fireplace. Without much persuasion, it is obvious that the pieces of coal belong to the red fiery heap in the fireplace, while we are content and safe sitting a few feet away within the reach of the coal's heat. What happens if we decide to change that state of equilibrium, say, by picking up a red hot piece of coal and dropping it on our laps? The results are obvious.

Now, think about the heated debates and arguments that you have watched on television or heard on the radio. Of course, seated on your cozy sofa a few feet from the television or radio it is easy to follow the debate, laugh about the antics of the debaters and possibly learn a lot from the debaters as they argue and debate some of the most controversial social issues. Some of these issues as was mentioned earlier include sexual aggression, aggression, sexual assault, sexual abuse, date rape, child labor, gender prejudice, racial prejudice, religious prejudice, abortion, animal cruelty, homosexuality, gun control, and death penalty. As much as you enjoy their debate from your comfy sofa, would you enjoy it as much if you invited the most argumentative of the debaters, the one who would not see reason, to your house to debate with you? Most likely not, because that will be like picking up the red hot coal described earlier and dropping it on your laps.

The two illustrations help drive home the point that controversial subjects or issues are best left out of daily conversations with the Know-It-All. This is emphatically true if the controversial issue is in the Know-It-All's domain of knowledge. Furthermore, remember that for some Know-It-Alls the hot controversial issues may not be the ones listed above. It might be the behavior of their son or daughter, or simply the way they drive recklessly or their shopping habits. So, identify the Know-It-All's hot controversial issues and stay away from them, don't drag and drop them into your daily conversation.

Walk away

Let's face it. Even after trying all the measures listed in this chapter, it is possible that the Know-It-All will not change his or her Know-It-All behaviors and actually may have stated verbally or by body language that he or she is not willing to make any change. In that case, you will need a unique solution different from the measures proffered in this chapter.

Keep in mind that prolonged and repeated exposure to the Know-It-All's behavior may lead to violence. Hence, one way to shut up or silence such an incorrigible Know-It-All is simply to walk away when they start to exhibit their Know-It-All behavior. This does not preclude salutation, exchange of pleasantries and normal conversation which is proper etiquette. However, you are now conscious not to allow yourself to be denigrated or humiliated by trying to reason or argue with the Know-It-All.

It is sincerely hoped that if you apply some of the measures outlined in this chapter it will help you curtail and or eliminate the denigrating influences of any Know-It-All who has caused you grief and irritation in the past.

Notes

Chapter 1
1. Sac.edu. "Controversial Issues." Web. January 17 2011<
http://www.sac.edu/students/library/nealley/websites/controversial.htm>
2. Kalton, Graham. Dr. Introduction to Survey Sampling. Newbury Park, California: Sage Publications Inc., 1983. pp. 5-7.
3. Kish, Leslie. Dr. Survey Sampling. New York: John Wiley and Sons, Inc., 1995. pp. 18
4. Cia.gov. "Central Intelligence Agency - The World Factbook." Web. January 17 2011
    <https://www.cia.gov/library/publications/the-world-factbook/fields/2098.html>
5. Hirsch, J.E. "An index to quantify an individual's scientific research output." November 2005. Web. January 16 2011 <http://www.pnas.org/content/102/46/16569.full>
6. Stringer, Michael, J. et.al. "Effectiveness of Journal Ranking Schemes as a Tool for Locating Information." February 2008. Web. January 16 2011 <http://www.plosone.org/article/info:doi/10.1371/journal.pone.0001683>
7. Google.com. "Technology overview." Web. January 16 2011
    <http://www.google.com/corporate/tech.html>
8. NIH.gov. "The Numbers Count: Mental Disorders in America." Web. January 17 2011
    <http://www.nimh.nih.gov/health/publications/the-numbers-count-mental-disorders-in-america/index.shtml>

Chapter 2
1. Tuttle, Brad. "The Customer Service Confrontation: What to Say to Get Fees Waived." February 2010. Web. December 15 2010 <http://money.blogs.time.com/2010/02/23/the-customer-service-confrontation-what-to-say-to-get-fees-waived>
2. Wade, John. "The know-it-all Syndrome". February 2005. Web. December 2 2010 <http://lifewise.canoe.ca/Living/2005/02/08/924273.html>
3. Dictionary.com, " Know-it-all." Web. December 2 2010 <http://dictionary.reference.com/browse/know-it-all>
4. Wiktionary.org, " Know-it-all." Web. December 2 2010 < http://en.wiktionary.org/wiki/know-it-all>
5. Blog/Forum Posting. "Why does my boyfriend always correct me / say I am wrong?" December 2008. Web. December 7 2010 <http://answers.yahoo.com/question/index?qid=20081008173034AAuXV8b>
6. Blog/Forum Posting. "My 8 year old is always correcting people!" December 2009. Web. December 7 2010 <http://www.focusonlinecommunities.com/message/83446>
7. Ludeman, Kate, and Erlandson, Eddie. Alpha Male Syndrome. Boston, Massachusetts: Harvard Business School Publishing, 2006. pp 126 -127.
8. Dictionary.com, " Pejorative." Web. December 2 2010 < http://dictionary.reference.com/browse/pejorative>

9. Romano, Andrew, "FINEMAN: Is Obama Playing It Too Cool?" September 2008. Web. December 14 2010 <http://www.newsweek.com/blogs/stumper/2008/09/19/fineman-is-obama-playing-it-too-cool.html>

10. Blog/Forum Posting. "Correcting people." September 2010. Web. December 7 2010
<http://www.psychforums.com/asperger-syndrome/topic54201.html>

11. Forward, Susan, and Frazier, Donna. Emotional Blackmail: When the People in Your Life Use Fear, Obligation, and Guilt to Manipulate You. New York: HarperCollins, 1998. pp. x.

12. Shenfeld, Hilary and Johnson, Dirk. "E-Mail: Before Clicking 'Send'..." May 2003. Web. December 16 2010
<http://www.newsweek.com/2003/05/18/e-mail-before-clicking- send.html>

13. Blog/Forum Posting. "Do people think you always have to be right?" January 2010. Web. December 7 2010
<http://www.psychforums.com/asperger-syndrome/topic46114.html>

14. behavenet.com. "Narcissistic Personality Disorder." Web. December 2 2010
<http://behavenet.com/capsules/disorders/narcissisticpd.htm>

15. Hollis, James, PH.D. Why Good People Do Bad Things - Understanding Our Darker Selves. London: Penguin Books Ltd., 2007. pp 94.

16. Blog/Forum Posting. "Why Does My Child Keep Correcting Me? - Asperger's Fear Monster #3." February 2008. Web. December 9 2010
<http://ezinearticles.com/?Why-Does-My-Child-Keep-Correcting-Me?---Aspergers-Fear-Monster-3&id=964962>

17. Blog/Forum Posting. "Asperger's syndrome." November 2010. Web. December 7 2010
<http://www.mayoclinic.com/health/aspergers-syndrome/DS00551>

18. Newsweek.com. "SCHOOLS: BATTLING 'E-BULLIES'." July 2005. Web. December 16

2010 <http://www.newsweek.com/2005/07/04/schools-battling-e-bullies.html>
19. Blog/Forum Posting. "Ways to communicate with a know-it-all." Web. December 16 2010
<http://www.helium.com/knowledge/55167-ways-to-communicate-with-a-know-it-all/>
20. Blog/Forum Posting. "How to deal with know-it-alls and annoying people." Web. December 16 2010 <http://www.helium.com/knowledge/5705-how-to-deal-with-know-it-alls-and-annoying-people/>

Chapter 3
1. merriam-webster.com, "Definition of KNOWLEDGE." Web. December 20 2010
<http://www.merriam-webster.com/dictionary/knowledge?show=0&t=1292862958>
2. Dictionary.com, "Conversation." Web. December 16 2010
<http://dictionary.reference.com/browse/conversation>
3. Blog/Forum Posting. "Online Conversation Starters." April 2010. Web. December 16 2010
<http://www.goconversation.com/category/online-conversation/>
4. Evans, Patricia. The Verbally Abusive Man - Can He Change? Avon, Massachusetts: Adams Media, 2006. pp 47.
5. Evans, Patricia. The Verbally Abusive Relationship: How to recognize it and how to respond. Avon, Massachusetts: Adams Media, 2010. pp 22.
6. chatfamily.com, "Chatroom Rules." Web. December 16 2010
<http://www.chatfamily.com/rules.html>
7. Lines, Dennis. The Bullies - Understanding Bullies and Bullying. London: Jessica

Kingsley Publishers, 2008. pp. 19.
8. Borda, Michelle, Ed.D. Nobody Likes Me, Everybody Hates Me. San Francisco: Jossey-Bass, 2005. pp 90.
9. Cohen, Adam. "New Laws Target Workplace Bullying." July 2010. Web. December 15 2010 <http://www.time.com/time/nation/article/0,8599,2005358,00.html>
10. Malamuth, Neil, M., and Thornhill, Nancy, W. "Hostile Masculinity, Sexual Aggression, and Gender-Biased Domineeringness in Conversations." Aggressive Behavior : Wiley-Liss, Inc. Journal 20 (1994): 185-193.
11. Geraci, Ron, and Swierczynski, Duane. "Talking yourself to death." Men's Health June 1997:
33. Academic Search Premier. EBSCO. DCCCD Library. 12 December 2010. <http://www.epnet.com/>.
12. Economist.com, "Chattering classes - The rules for verbal exchanges are surprisingly enduring." December 2006. Web. December 16 2010. <http://www.economist.com/node/8345491?story_id=8345491>
13. Dictionary.com, "Speech." Web. December 16 2010 <http://dictionary.reference.com/browse/speech>
14. Evans, Patricia. Controlling People: How to Recognize, Understand, and Deal with People Who Try to Control You. Avon, Massachusetts: Adams Media, 2002. pp 3, 150.
15. Vaid, J., V. S. Ramachandran, V.S. "Laughter and humour." Web. December 20 2010
<http://www.answers.com/topic/laughter-and-humour>
16. Masters, Brooke, A. "Is Email Harassment Illegal?" November 1998. Web. December 15 2010 <http://www.washingtonpost.com/wp-srv/local/frompost/nov98/email01.htm>
17. Macdonald, Lynda. Tolley's Managing Email & Internet Use. London: Reed Elsevier

(UK) Ltd, 2004. pp 6.
18. Newsweek.com. "SCHOOLS: BATTLING 'E-BULLIES'." July 2005. Web. December 16 2010 <http://www.newsweek.com/2005/07/04/schools-battling-e-bullies.html>
19. Leggatt, Helen. "Nielsen Mobile: Texting vs. talking." September 2008. Web. December 20 2010 <http://www.bizreport.com/2008/09/nielsen_mobile_texting_vs_talking.html>
20. Tschabitscher, Heinz. "How Many Emails Are Sent Every Day?." Web. December 20 2010
    <http://email.about.com/od/emailtrivia/f/emails_per_day.htm>
21. Watson, Robert. "Email Abuse - How to Stop Online Harassment." July 2007. Web. December 15   2010 <http://www.associatedcontent.com/article/291034/email_abuse_how_to
    _stop_online_harassment.html?cat=35>
22. Criminaldefenselawyer.com. "Email Harassment." Web. December 15 2010
    <http://www.criminaldefenselawyer.com/info/email-harassment>
23. Kim, Claudia. "Is Email Harassment Illegal?" Web. December 15 2010
    <http://ezinearticles.com/?Is-Email-Harassment-Illegal?&id=1465539>
24. Blog/Forum Posting. "Ladies do you always correct you husband." May 2009. Web. December 7 2010 <http://www.answerology.com/index.aspx/question/2660448_ladies-do-you-always-correct-you-husband.html>
25. Blog/Forum Posting. "Correcting mistakes." August 2010. Web. December 7 2010
    <http://thechatpage.com/Archive/CorrectingMistakes/gzdhm/post.htm>

26. Carnegie Mellon CyLab Information Networking Institute, "Instant Messaging and Chat." Web. December 16 2010 <http://www.mysecurecyberspace.com/secure/instant-messaging-and-chat.html>
27. Blog/Forum Posting. "You remind me of my sister, always correcting my grammar." December 2008. Web. December 7 2010 <http://www.huffingtonpost.com/social/ bwalsh1/bill-ayers-on-hardball-ca_n_150079_18702688.html>
28. Blog/Forum Posting. "HARMLESS THOUGHTS." November 2003. Web. December 2 2010 <http://blog.harmlessonline.net/2003/11/personality-abnormalities-2.html>
29. Blog/Forum Posting. "Correcting Others Makes YOU Look Bad." February 2009. Web. December 7 2010 <http://blog.jvf.com/2009/02/10/correcting-others-makes-you-look-bad>
30. Blog/Forum Posting. "Correcting people - especially older people." May 2008. Web. December 7 2010 <http://community.livejournal.com/etiquetteworld/44551.html>
31. Carver, Mike. "If I Had My Career to Do Over Again . . .Mike Carver's Top 10 List." May 2008. Web. December 2 2010 <http://www.aami.org/career/resources/development/2008.05.carverstopten.html>
32. Cohen, Adam. "New Laws Target Workplace Bullying." July 2010. Web. December 15 2010 <http://www.time.com/time/nation/article/0,8599,2005358,00.html>
33. Thomas, Evans, "I Am Addicted To Prescription Pain Medication." October 2003. Web. December 14 2010 <http://www.newsweek.com/2003/10/19/i-am-addicted-to-prescription-pain-medication.html>

Chapter 4

1. Dictionary.com. "Backseat driver." Web. December 22 2010 <http://dictionary.reference.com/browse/backseat+driver+>
2. Groh-Gordy, Michelle. "Perfecting the art of being a backseat driver." August 2006. Web. December 22 2010 <http://www.sbsun.com/columnists/ci_4177255>
3. Encarta.msn.com. "Armchair quarterback." Web. December 22 2010 <http://encarta.msn.com/dictionary_561535560/armchair_quarterback.html>
4. Blog/Forum Posting. "Correcting Others Makes YOU Look Bad." February 2009. Web. December 7 2010 <http://blog.jvf.com/2009/02/10/correcting-others-makes-you-look-bad>
5. Young, Katie. "That Know-it-all Jerk At Work." July 2007. Web. December 22 2010 <http://www.midweek.com/content/columns/theyoungview_article/that_know_it_all_jerk_at_work/>
6. CorporationCentre.ca. "How to Deal with the Know-It-All Employee." February 2010. Web. December 22 2010 <http://corpcentre.blogspot.com/2010/02/how-to-deal-with-know-it-all-employee.html>
7. Schroeder, Daniel, Ph.D. "Human Resources: Know-it-all' employee needs 'crucial conversation'." May 2005. Web. December 22 2010 <http://www.biztimes.com/news/2005/5/27/human-resources-know-it-all-employee-needs-crucial-conversation>
8. Dictionary.com. "Boss." Web. December 22 2010 <http://dictionary.reference.com/browse/boss>
9. Chen, Serena, and Fast, Nathanael, "The Making of a Toxic Boss." October 2009. Web. December 14 2010 <http://www.newsweek.com/2009/10/18/the-making-of-a-toxic-boss.html/>

10. Cohen, Adam. "New Laws Target Workplace Bullying." July 2010. Web. December 15 2010 <http://www.time.com/time/nation/article/0,8599,2005358,00.html>
11. Blog/Forum Posting. "Know-it-all." April 2010. Web. December 2 2010
<http://everything2.com/title/know-it-all>
12. Blog/Forum Posting. "(Don't) Correct Me If I'm Wrong." July 2007. Web. December 9 2010
<http://spectatrix.com/2007/07/29/dont-correct-me-if-im-wrong/>
13. Blog/Forum Posting. "Teachers always humiliating me?" December 2008. Web. December 10 2010 <http://answers.yahoo.com/question/index?qid=20080701084353AA8EGe5>
14. Lindner, Evelin Ph.D. "I Never Thought of Humiliation. Why?" The Psychology of Humiliation: A Journal: A Susmita Thukral Journal Fall (2004): 2.
15. Buzzle.com. "What Makes a Good Teacher." Web. December 22 2010
<http://www.buzzle.com/articles/what-makes-a-good-teacher.html>
16. Blog/Forum Posting. "Other What are your thoughts on students "correcting" teachers?" March 2010. Web. December 7 2010 <http://www.proteacher.net/discussions/showthread.php?t=236534>
17. Ludeman, Kate, and Erlandson, Eddie. Alpha Male Syndrome. Boston, Massachusetts: Harvard Business School Publishing, 2006. pp. 126.
18. Borda, Michelle, Ed.D. Nobody Likes Me, Everybody Hates Me. San Francisco:
    Jossey- Bass, 2005. pp. 90.
19. Jacobs, Judge, T. Teen Cyberbullying Investigated - Where Do Your Rights End and

Consequences Begin? Minneapolis, Minesota: Free Spirit Publishing, Inc., 2010. pp. xi.
20. Newsweek.com. "SCHOOLS: BATTLING 'E-BULLIES'." July 2005. Web. December 16 2010 <http://www.newsweek.com/2005/07/04/schools-battling-e-bullies.html>
21. Blog/Forum Posting. "Woman grows weary of boyfriend always correcting her." January 2010. Web. December 7 2010 <http://www.adn.com/2010/01/14/1094307/woman-grows-weary-of-boyfriend.html>
22. Blog/Forum Posting. "He is always correcting me but I don't want to hurt his feelings by saying something." January 2010. Web. December 7 2010
    <http://www.dearcupid.org/question/he-is-always-correcting-me-but-i-dont.html>
23. Blog/Forum Posting. "Always Criticizing Me." November 2008. Web. December 7 2010
    <http://savingamarriagehelp.com/always-criticizing-me/>
24. Blog/Forum Posting. "Why is it the my girlfriend is always correcting everyone including
    me?." April 2010. Web. December 7 2010 <http://answers.yahoo.com/question/index?qid=
    20100415054131AA7U9F8>
25. Blog/Forum Posting. "So my girlfriend is always correcting me?" June 2010. Web. December 7 2010 <http://ca.answers.yahoo.com/question/index?qid=
    20100618084318AA1u65Q>
26. Reynolds, Gillian. "Warning Signs That Your Husband Has a Girlfriend." Web. December 22 2010 <http://ezinearticles.com/?Warning-Signs-That-Your-Husband-Has-a-Girlfriend &id=1040564>
27. Blog/Forum Posting. "My husband makes me feel stupid and unwanted." September 2009.

Web. December 7 2010 <http://www.oprah.com/community/thread/116987>

28. Blog/Forum Posting. "What would you do if your spouse was always correcting you?" October 2008. Web. December 7 2010 <http://www.whatsyourconundrum.com/love-and-relationships /what-would-you-do-if-your-spouse-was-always-correcting-you>

29. Blog/Forum Posting. " My Know It All Boyfriend The Ways I Deal With It" September 2009. Web. December 2 2010 <http://hubpages.com/hub/My-Know-It-All-Boyfriend-The-Ways-I-Deal-With-It>

30. Blog/Forum Posting. "Good posts Mjegan. My wife is always correcting me with the kids and it drives me nuts. She is learning, though." June 2010. Web. December 7 2010
<http://www.huffingtonpost.com/social/KennyFox/fathers-day-dads-not-just_b_615303
_51016585.html>

31. Blog/Forum Posting. "Do people think you always have to be right?" January 2010. Web. December 7 2010 <http://www.psychforums.com/asperger-syndrome/topic46114.html>

32. Blog/Forum Posting. "I am always anxious and depressed around my best friend." September 2009. Web. December 7 2010 <http://isitnormal.com/story/i-am-always-anxious-and-depressed-around-my-best-friend-39715/>

33. Blog/Forum Posting. "How do I tell my friend that she is so irritating. She always think she's right?" December 2008. Web. December 7 2010<http://sg.answers.yahoo.com/question/ index?qid=20080730030851AACHShv>

34. Gurgle.com. "The know-it-all mum." Web. December 24 2010
　　<http://www.gurgle.com/articles/Lifestyle/36805/The_know_it_all_mum.aspx>
35. Blog/Forum Posting. "My mom makes me hate myself." March 2010. Web. December 7 2010 <http://www.socialanxietysupport.com/forum/f26/my-mom-makes-me-hate-myself-85993/>
36. Blog/Forum Posting. "How to resolve problems with an interfering mother in law and a know it all father in law?." Web. December 25 2010 <http://answers.yahoo.com/question/index?qid=20061225165528AAHBSsI>
37. Zamora, Dulce. "Men die at higher rates than women for all of the top 10 causes of death. Why don't men take better care of their health?" Web. December 25 2010
　　<http://men.webmd.com/features/mens-top-5-health-concerns>
38. Blog/Forum Posting. "How do I deal with a know it all boyfriend?" Web. December 26 2010
　　<http://answers.yahoo.com/question/index?qid=20080110140904AAv8AXO>
39. Lilley, Roy. Dealing with Difficult People. London: Kogan Page, 2004. pp 13.
40. McKelden, Shannon. "The Know-it-All Stage - The Good, the Bad and How to Keep Your Sanity." Web. December 26 2010 <http://www.childrentoday.com/articles/discipline/the-know-it-all-stage-4550/>
41. Lehman, James. ""I'm Right and You're Wrong!" Is Your Child a Know-it-all?" Web. December 26 2010 <http://www.empoweringparents.com/arguing-with-your-opinionated-child.php#>
42. Blog/Forum Posting. "Why Does My Child Keep Correcting Me? - Asperger's Fear Monster

#3." February 2008. Web. December 9 2010 <http://ezinearticles.com/?Why-Does-My-Child-Keep-Correcting-Me?---Aspergers-Fear-Monster-3&id=964962>

43. Blog/Forum Posting. "My 8 year old is always correcting people!" December 2009. Web. December 7 2010 <http://www.focusonlinecommunities.com/message/83446>

44. Blog/Forum Posting. "You remind me of my sister, always correcting my grammar." December 2008. Web. December 7 2010 <http://www.huffingtonpost.com/social/bwalsh1/bill-ayers-on-hardball-ca_n_150079_18702688.html>

45. DrPhil.com. "Sibling Rivalry." Web. December 26 2010 <http://www.drphil.com/shows/show/43/>

46. Lewis, Leo. "Chat room bullies face end to their internet anonymity." June 2007. Web. December 27 2010 <http://www.timesonline.co.uk/tol/news/world/asia/article2005592.ece>

47. Gerber, Lauren. "Fake Profiles On Fakebook/Facebook!" October 2008. Web. December 27 2010 <http://www.pc1news.com/news/0325/fake-profiles-on-fakebook-facebook.html>

48. Grove, Jennifer, V. "4 Teens Sued for Obscene Fake Facebook Profile." Web. December 27 2010 <http://mashable.com/2009/09/25/fake-facebook-profile/>

Chapter 5

1. Blog/Forum Posting. "Controversial Conversation Topics." March 2009. Web. December 16 2010 <http://www.goconversation.com/controversial-conversation-topics/>

Chapter 6
1. itstime.com, Online Newsletter. "Dealing with Difficult People." March 1999. Web. December 2 2010 <http://www.itstime.com/mar99.htm>
2. Isaacs, Florence. Toxic Friends - True Friends. New York: William Morrow and Company, Inc., 1999. pp. xv.
3. Leibling, Mike. How People Tick - A guide to over 50 types of difficult people and how to handle them. London: Kogan Page, 2009. pp. 1-208.
4. Blog/Forum Posting. " How can I stop being a know-it-all?" October 2006. Web. December 16 2010 < http://ask.metafilter.com/48541/How-can-I-stop-being-a-knowitall>
5. Blog/Forum Posting. "How can I get my husband to stop always correcting me?." December 2005. Web. December 7 2010 <http://answers.yahoo.com/question/index?qid=1006021013511>
6. Blog/Forum Posting. "Correcting Others Makes YOU Look Bad." February 2009. Web. December 7 2010 <http://blog.jvf.com/2009/02/10/correcting-others-makes-you-look-bad>
7. Blog/Forum Posting. "I am always anxious and depressed around my best friend." September 2009. Web. December 7 2010 <http://isitnormal.com/story/i-am-always-anxious-and-depressed-around-my-best-friend-39715/>
8. Blog/Forum Posting. "Correcting people." September 2010. Web. December 7 2010
 <http://www.psychforums.com/asperger-syndrome/topic54201.html>
9. May, Larry. "Insensitivity and moral responsibility." The Journal of Value Inquiry : A
 SpringerLink Journal 26 (1992): 7-22.

10. Barry, Brian, P. "Extremity of vice and the character of evil." The Journal of Philosophical Research : A Saginaw Valley State University Journal 35 (2010): 28.
11. Scott, Michelle. " Narcissistic Personality Disorder: It's All About Me, Didn't You Know?" November 2008. Web. December 7 2010 <http://www.associatedcontent.com/article/ 1163474/narcissistic_personality_disorder_its.html?cat=70>
12. Blog/Forum Posting. "How do you approach a family member that has a superiority complex?" December 2008. Web. December 12 2010 <http://answers.yahoo.com/question/index?qid=20090322180350AAwQH2P>
13. Malamuth, Neil, M., and Thornhill, Nancy, W. "Hostile Masculinity, Sexual Aggression, and
Gender-Biased Domineeringness in Conversations." Aggressive Behavior : Wiley-Liss, Inc. Journal 20 (1994): 185-193.
14. Blog/Forum Posting. "10 Tips for Effective Conversation." April 2008. Web. December 12 2010
<http://www.srichinmoybio.co.uk/blog/communication/10-tips-for-effective-conversation/>
15. Wohlfeil, Carol. " Ways to communicate with a know-it-all." Web. December 2 2010
< http://www.helium.com/items/293575-ways-to-communicate-with-a-know-it-all>
16. Menninger, Karl. The Human Mind. New York: Alfred A. Knopf, Inc., 1971. pp. 74.
17. Adler, Alfred. Josef Rattner. New York: Frederick Ungar Publishing Co., 1983. pp. 147.
18. Campbell, Anne. Men, Women, and Aggression - From Rage in Marriage to Violence in the Streets - How Gender Affects the Way We Act. New York: HarperCollins Publishers, 1993. pp. 73.

19. Ludeman, Kate, and Erlandson, Eddie. Alpha Male Syndrome. Boston, Massachusetts: Harvard Business School Publishing, 2006. pp. 126.
20. Hamilton, Anita. "50 Best Websites 2008." Web. December 15 2010
<http://www.time.com/time/specials/2007/article/0,28804,1809858_1809956_1811540,00.html>
21. Lilley, Roy. Dealing with Difficult People. London: Kogan Page, 2004. pp 13.
22. Zukav, Gary, and Francis, Linda. The Heart of the Soul - Emotional Awareness. New York: Simon & Schuster Source, 2001. pp. 132.
23. Cava, Roberta. Dealing with Difficult People - How to Deal with Nasty Customers, Demanding Bosses and Annoying Co-workers. New York: Firefly Books, 2004. pp. 94.
24. Blog/Forum Posting. "(Don't) Correct Me If I'm Wrong." July 2007. Web. December 9 2010
<http://spectatrix.com/2007/07/29/dont-correct-me-if-im-wrong/>
25. Viscott, David, M.D. Emotional Resilience - Simple Truths for Dealing with the Unfinished Business of Your Past. New York: Harmony Books, 1996. pp. 242.
26. Allport, Gordon. The Nature of Prejudice. New York: Perseus Books Publishing, L.L.C., 1979. pp. 382.
27. Hollis, James, PH.D. Why Good People Do Bad Things - Understanding Our Darker Selves. London: Penguin Books Ltd., 2007. pp. 104.
28. Isaacs, Florence. Toxic Friends - True Friends. New York: William Morrow and Company, Inc., 1999. pp. 56.
29. Corey, Gerald, and Corey, Marianne, S. I Never Knew I Had a Choice. Pacific Grove, California: Brooks/Cole Publishing Company, 2007. pp. 222.

30. McCoy, Dorothy, Ed.D. The Manipulative Man: Identify His Behavior, Counter the Abuse, Regain Control. Avon, Massachusetts: Adams Media, Inc., 2006. pp. 3.
31. Bolton, Robert, Ph.D. People Skills: how to assert yourself, listen to others, and resolve conflicts. New York: Simon & Schuster, Inc., 1979. pp. 15.
32. Blog/Forum Posting. "Always Criticizing Me." November 2008. Web. December 7 2010
   <http://savingamarriagehelp.com/always-criticizing-me/>
33. Evans, Patricia. The Verbally Abusive Relationship: How to recognize it and how to respond. Avon, Massachusetts: Adams Media, 2010. pp. 10.
34. Gesaman, Krista. "Abuse of Power." January 2010. Web. December 14 2010
   <http://www.newsweek.com/2010/01/12/abuse-of-power.html/>
35. Brownell, Judy. Listening - Attitudes, Principles, and Skills. Boston: Pearson Education Inc., 2010. pp. 85.
36. thesaurus.com. "Know It All." January 2010. Web. December 2 2010
   < http://thesaurus.com/browse/know+it+all>
37. Horney, Karen. Self Analysis. New York: W.W. Norton & Company Inc., 1942. pp. 41.
38. Adler, Alfred. Josef Rattner. New York: Frederick Ungar Publishing Co., 1983. pp. 155.
39. Feinberg, Mortimer, PH.D., and Tarrant, John, J. Why Smart People Do Dumb Things. New York: Simon & Schuster Inc., 1995. pp. 74.
40. Wade, John. "The know-it-all Syndrome". February 2005. Web. December 2 2010
   <http://lifewise.canoe.ca/Living/2005/02/08/924273.html>
41. Blog/Forum Posting. "Ladies do you always correct you husband." May 2009. Web. December 7 2010

<http://www.answerology.com/index.aspx/question/2660448_ladies-do-you-always-correct-you-husband.html>
42. Corey, Gerald, and Corey, Marianne, S. I Never Knew I Had a Choice. Pacific Grove, California: Brooks/Cole Publishing Company, 2007. pp. 285.
43. Puhn, Laurie, J.D. Instant Persuassion. New York: Tarcher/Penguin, 2005. pp. 253 -256.
44. Ludeman, Kate, and Erlandson, Eddie. Alpha Male Syndrome. Boston, Massachusetts: Harvard Business School Publishing, 2006. pp. 127.
45. Blog/Forum Posting. " My Know It All Boyfriend The Ways I Deal With It." Web. December 2 2010 <http://hubpages.com/hub/My-Know-It-All-Boyfriend-The-Ways-I-Deal-With-It >
46. Courtney, Donald. "Ways to communicate with a know-it-all." Web. December 2 2010 <http://www.helium.com/items/873338-ways-to-communicate-with-a-know-it-all >
47. Evans, Patricia. Controlling People: How to Recognize, Understand, and Deal with People Who Try to Control You. Avon, Massachusetts: Adams Media, 2002. pp. 184.
48. Bolton, Robert, Ph.D. People Skills: how to assert yourself, listen to others, and resolve conflicts. New York: Simon & Schuster, Inc., 1979. pp. 12.
49. Fromm, Erich. The Anatomy of Human Destructiveness. Canada: Holt, Rinehart and Winston of Canada, Limited, 1973. pp. 201.
50. Evans, Patricia. Controlling People: How to Recognize, Understand, and Deal with People Who Try to Control You. Avon, Massachusetts: Adams Media, 2002. pp 3, 150.
51. Blog/Forum Posting. "'I Know it All' Syndrome." June 2009. Web. December 2 2010 < http://losttext.com/2009/06/i-know-it-all-syndrome/ >

52. Cava, Roberta. Dealing with Difficult People - How to Deal with Nasty Customers, Demanding Bosses and Annoying Co-workers. New York: Firefly Books, 2004. pp. 88.
53. Dictionary.com. "Obnoxious." Web. December 27 2010
    <http://dictionary.reference.com/browse/Obnoxious+>
54. Gray, Paul. "Books: Backwaters and Eccentrics." February 1982. Web. December 15 2010
    <http://www.time.com/time/magazine/article/0,9171,922774,00.html>
55. Viscott, David, M.D. Emotional Resilience - Simple Truths for Dealing with the Unfinished Business of Your Past. New York: Harmony Books, 1996. pp. 241.
56. haltabuse.org. "WHO@ - Working to Halt Online Abuse." Web. December 16 2010
    <http://www.haltabuse.org/help/isit.shtml>
57. Huang, Paul. "E-mail Harassment." Web. December 15 2010
    <http://www.files.chem.vt.edu/chem-dept/dessy/honors/papers/huang.html>
58. Alexandria, Donna. "Ways to communicate with a know-it-all." Web. January 04 2011
    < http://www.helium.com/items/293907-ways-to-communicate-with-a-know-it-all >

Chapter 7
1. Blog/Forum Posting, "Know-it-all." April 2010. Web. December 2 2010
    <http://everything2.com/title/know-it-all>
2. Blog/Forum Posting, "Why is it the my girlfriend is always correcting everyone including me?." April 2010. Web. December 7 2010
    <http://answers.yahoo.com/question/index?qid=20100415054131AA7U9F8>

3. Blog/Forum Posting, "Always Criticizing Me." November 2008. Web. December 7 2010
<http://savingamarriagehelp.com/always-criticizing-me/>
4. Zukav, Gary, and Francis, Linda. The Heart of the Soul - Emotional Awareness. New York: Simon & Schuster Source, 2001. pp. 132.
5. Scrubsmag.com. "How do I deal with know-it-all colleagues?" May 2009. Web. January 04 2011 <http://scrubsmag.com/how-to-deal-with-a-know-it-all-colleague/>
6. Webber, Bridget. "How to deal with a know-it-all at work." Web. January 04 2011 <http://www.helium.com/items/1815468-how-to-deal-with-a-know-it-all-at-work>
7. Crumley, Bruce. "French Bid to Ban Marital Abuse That's Psychological." January 2010. Web. December 15 2010 <http://www.time.com/time/world/article/0,8599,1952552,00.html>
8. Cava, Roberta. Dealing with Difficult People - How to Deal with Nasty Customers, Demanding Bosses and Annoying Co-workers. New York: Firefly Books, 2004. pp. 94.
9. Ketterman, Grace, M.D. Verbal Abuse Healing the Hidden Wound. Ann Habor Michigan: Servant Publications, 1992. pp. 13.
10. O'Toole, Jay. "Ways to communicate with a know-it-all." Web. December 2 2010
< http://www.helium.com/items/290777-ways-to-communicate-with-a-know-it-all>
11. Zukav, Gary, and Francis, Linda. The Heart of the Soul - Emotional Awareness. New York: Simon & Schuster Source, 2001. pp. 137.
12. Ellison, Sharon, S. Taking the War Out of our Words - The Art of Powerful Non-Defensive Communication. Berkeley, California: Bay Tree Publishing, 2002. pp. 7.

13. Cava, Roberta. Dealing with Difficult People - How to Deal with Nasty Customers, Demanding Bosses and Annoying Co-workers. New York: Firefly Books, 2004. pp. 94.
14. Blog/Forum Posting, "I am always anxious and depressed around my best friend." September 2009. Web. December 7 2010 <http://isitnormal.com/story/i-am-always-anxious-and-depressed-around-my-best-friend-39715/>
15. Blog/Forum Posting, "(Don't) Correct Me If I'm Wrong." July 2007. Web. December 9 2010
<http://spectatrix.com/2007/07/29/dont-correct-me-if-im-wrong/>
16. Blog/Forum Posting. "Are people intimidated by intelligence?" Web. January 04 2011
<http://answers.yahoo.com/question/index?qid=20090202180123AA0ic6T>
17. Govind, Das. "Ways to communicate with a know-it-all." Web. January 04 2011
<http://www.helium.com/items/1733672-ways-to-communicate-with-a-know-it-all>
18. Blog/Forum Posting. " My Know It All Boyfriend The Ways I Deal With It" September 2009. Web. December 2 2010 <http://hubpages.com/hub/My-Know-It-All-Boyfriend-The-Ways-I-Deal-With-It>
19. Corey, Gerald, and Corey, Marianne, S. I Never Knew I Had a Choice. Pacific Grove, California: Brooks/Cole Publishing Company, 2007. pp. 222.
20. Can, Tran. "Ways to communicate with a know-it-all." Web. January 04 2011
< http://www.helium.com/items/1236964-ways-to-communicate-with-a-know-it-all>
21. McCoy, Dorothy, Ed.D. The Manipulative Man: Identify His Behavior, Counter the Abuse, Regain Control. Avon, Massachusetts: Adams Media, Inc., 2006. pp. 3.

22. Alexandria, Donna. "Ways to communicate with a know-it-all." Web. January 04 2011
    < http://www.helium.com/items/293907-ways-to-communicate-with-a-know-it-all >
23. Blog/Forum Posting, "So my girlfriend is always correcting me?" June 2010. Web. December 7 2010 <http://ca.answers.yahoo.com/question/index?qid=20100618084318AA1u65Q>
24. Kazay, Ginger. "Ways to communicate with a know-it-all." Web. January 04 2011
    < http://www.helium.com/items/290437-ways-to-communicate-with-a-know-it-all>
25. Blog/Forum Posting. " How do i get my know-it-all, nit-picking boyfriend to leave me alone in the kitchen?" Web. January 04 2011
    <http://answers.yahoo.com/question/index?qid=20101123165755AAfQbDs>
26. Blog/Forum Posting, "Nitpicking, finding errors and correcting." September 2008. Web. December 7 2010 <http://forums.plentyoffish.com/datingPosts10862186.aspx>
27. Hayden, Scott. "How to Deal With Know-It-All Personalities." December 2009. Web. December 2 2010 <http://www.suite101.com/content/how-to-deal-with-knowitall-personalities-a182170>
28. Hunt, Jane. " About Office Bullies." December 2009. Web. January 5 2011
    <http://www.ehow.com/about_4780588_office-bullies.html>
29. Blog/Forum Posting, "Woman grows weary of boyfriend always correcting her." January 2010. Web. December 7 2010
    <http://www.adn.com/2010/01/14/1094307/woman-grows-weary-of-boyfriend.html>
30. Strongman, K.T. The Psychology of Emotion - From Everyday Life to Theory. Sussex,

England: John Wiley & Sons Ltd., 2003. pp. 147-148.
31. Blog/Forum Posting, "Correcting people." September 2010. Web. December 7 2010
 <http://www.psychforums.com/asperger-syndrome/topic54201.html>
32. Blog/Forum Posting. "Why do many women who answer questions on this site come off as obnoxious know it all snobs?" Web. January 6 2011
 <http://answers.yahoo.com/question/index?qid=20070507064538AAKli9p>
33. Blog/Forum Posting, "What can you do …?" Web. December 7 2010
 <http://wiki.answers.com/Q/What_can_you_do_when_your_teacher_is_British_and_is_always_correcting_me_and_embarrassing_people_in_front_of_the_class_and_picks_favorites_and_each_time_I_see_her_I_feel_like_hitting_her>
34. Blog/Forum Posting, "(Don't) Correct Me If I'm Wrong." July 2007. Web. December 9 2010
 <http://spectatrix.com/2007/07/29/dont-correct-me-if-im-wrong/>
35. Corey, Gerald, and Corey, Marianne, S. I Never Knew I Had a Choice. Pacific Grove, California: Brooks/Cole Publishing Company, 2007. pp. 285.
36. Jung, Carl, G. The Undiscovered Self. Boston: Atlantic Monthly Press - Little, Brown and Company, 1957. pp. 104-105.
37. Blog/Forum Posting, "Teachers always humiliating me?" December 2008. Web. December 10 2010 <http://answers.yahoo.com/question/index?qid=20080701084353AA8EGe5>
38. Lindner, Evelin Ph.D. "I Never Thought of Humiliation. Why ?" The Psychology of Humiliation : A Journal: A Susmita Thukral Journal Fall (2004): 2.
39. Cohen, Adam. "New Laws Target Workplace Bullying." July 2010. Web. December 15 2010

<http://www.time.com/time/nation/article/0,8599,2005358,00.html>

Chapter 8
1. Wood, Samuel, E et al. The World of Psychology. Boston: Pearson Education Inc., 2008. pp. 556.
2. May, Larry. "Insensitivity and moral responsibility." The Journal of Value Inquiry : A SpringerLink Journal 26 (1992): 7-22.
3. Barry, Brian, P. "Extremity of vice and the character of evil." The Journal of Philosophical Research : A Saginaw Valley State University Journal 35 (2010): 28.
4. Dictionary.com, "Insecure." Web. January 07 2011
    <http://dictionary.reference.com/browse/Insecure>
5. Adler, Alfred. Josef Rattner. New York: Frederick Ungar Publishing Co., 1983. pp. 147.
6. Chen, Serena, and Fast, Nathanael, "The Making of a Toxic Boss." October 2009. Web. December 14 2010 <http://www.newsweek.com/2009/10/18/the-making-of-a-toxic-boss.html/>
7. Cohen, Adam. "New Laws Target Workplace Bullying." July 2010. Web. December 15 2010
    <http://www.time.com/time/nation/article/0,8599,2005358,00.html>
8. Wood, Samuel, E et al. The World of Psychology. Boston: Pearson Education Inc., 2008. pp. 514.
9. Feinberg, Mortimer, PH.D., and Tarrant, John, J. Why Smart People Do Dumb Things. New York: Simon & Schuster Inc., 1995. pp. 74.
10. Fromm, Erich. The Anatomy of Human Destructiveness. Canada: Holt, Rinehart and Winston of Canada, Limited, 1973. pp. 201.
11. Puhn, Laurie, J.D. Instant Persuassion. New York: Tarcher/Penguin, 2005. pp. 253.
12. Corey, Gerald, and Corey, Marianne, S. I Never Knew I Had a Choice. Pacific Grove,

California: Brooks/Cole Publishing Company, 2007. pp.285.
13. Wood, Samuel, E et al. The World of Psychology. Boston: Pearson Education Inc., 2008. pp. 467.
14. Adler, Alfred. Josef Rattner. New York: Frederick Ungar Publishing Co., 1983. pp. 155.
15. Menninger, Karl. The Human Mind. New York: Alfred A. Knopf, Inc., 1971. pp. 74.
16. Rottenberg, Julie. "How Do You Deal With Conversation Dominators?" Web. December 12 2010 <http://www.realsimple.com/worklife/etiquette/manners/how-to-deal-with-people-who-dominate-conversation-00000000027497/index.html>
17. Harrell, Keith. Attitude is Everything - 10 Life Changing Steps To Turning Attitude Into Action. New York: HarperCollins Publishers Inc., 2000.
18. Horney, Karen. Self Analysis. New York: W.W. Norton & Company Inc., 1942. pp. 41.
19. Zukav, Gary, and Francis, Linda. The Heart of the Soul - Emotional Awareness. New York: Simon & Schuster Source, 2001. pp. 163.
20. Lavelle, Jon. Water Off a Duck's Back: How to Deal with Frustrating Situations, Awkward, Exasperating and Manipulative People and... Keep Smiling! Great Britian: Blue Ice Publishing, 2008. pp. 18.
21. McCoy, Dorothy, Ed.D. The Manipulative Man: Identify His Behavior, Counter the Abuse, Regain Control. Avon, Massachusetts: Adams Media, Inc., 2006. pp. 3.
22. Evans, Patricia. Controlling People: How to Recognize, Understand, and Deal with People Who Try to Control You. Avon, Massachusetts: Adams Media, 2002. pp. 150.
23. Losttext.com, " 'I Know it All' Syndrome." June 2009. Web. January 07 2011

< http://losttext.com/2009/06/i-know-it-all-syndrome/>

24. Brownell, Judy. Listening - Attitudes, Principles, and Skills. Boston: Pearson Education Inc., 2010. pp. 85-86.

25. Nichols, Michael, D., PH.D. The Lost Art of Listening. New York: The Guilford Press, 1995. pp. 10.

26. Beier, Ernst, G. Dr. and Valens, Evans, G. People Reading - How We Control Others, How They Control Us. Lanham, Maryland: Scarborough House, 1992. pp. 28.

27. Puhn, Laurie, J.D. Instant Persuassion. New York: Tarcher/Penguin, 2005. pp. 66.

28. ibid. pp. 256.

29. Chinmoy, Sri. "10 Tips for Effective Conversation." April 2008. Web. December 12 2010
<http://www.srichinmoybio.co.uk/blog/communication/10-tips-for-effective-conversation/>

30. Tracy, Brian. "Sharpening Your Conversation Skills." Web. December 12 2010
<http://personal-development.com/brian-tracy-articles/sharpen-conversation-skills.htm/>

31. Geraci, Ron, and Swierczynski, Duane. "Talking yourself to death." Men's Health June 1997:
33. Academic Search Premier. EBSCO. DCCCD Library. 12 December 2010. <http://www.epnet.com/>.

32. Patterson, Kerry et al. Crucial Conversations: tools for talking when stakes are high. New York: McGraw-Hill, 2002. pp. 48.

33. Sternberg, Robert, J. Successful Intelligence - How Practical and Creative Intelligence Determine Success In Life. New York: Simon & Schuster Inc., 1996. pp. 255.

34. ibid. pp. 263.

35. Donaldson, Charlie et al. Stop Hurting the Woman You Love - Breaking the Cycle of

Abusive Behavior. Center City, Minnesota: Hazelden, 2006. pp. 3.

36. Gesaman, Krista. "Abuse of Power." January 2010. Web. December 14 2010
<http://www.newsweek.com/2010/01/12/abuse-of-power.html/>

37. Borda, Michelle, Ed.D. Nobody Likes Me, Everybody Hates Me. San Francisco: Jossey-Bass, 2005. pp. 90.

38. Puhn, Laurie, J.D. Instant Persuassion. New York: Tarcher/Penguin, 2005. pp. 4-6.

39. Ludeman, Kate, and Erlandson, Eddie. Alpha Male Syndrome. Boston,
   Massachusetts: Harvard Business School Publishing, 2006. pp. 126.

Chapter 9

1. Lavelle, Jon. Water Off a Duck's Back: How to Deal with Frustrating Situations, Awkward, Exasperating and Manipulative People and... Keep Smiling! Great Britian: Blue Ice Publishing, 2008. pp. 18.

2. Dictionary.com. "Shut up." Web. January 10 2011
   <http://dictionary.reference.com/browse/shut+up>

3. Blog/Forum Posting, "What would you do if your spouse was always correcting you?" October 2008. Web. December 7 2010
<http://www.whatsyourconundrum.com/love-and-relationships/what-would-you-do-if-your-spouse-was-always-correcting-you>

4. McClure, Lynne, Ph.D. Angry Women - Stop Letting Anger Control Your Life. Manassas Park, Virginia: Impact Publications, 2004. pp. 55.

5. Branden, Nathaniel. The Six Pillars of Self Esteem. New York: Bantam Book, 1994. pp. 26-27

6. Blog/Forum Posting, "Ladies do you always correct you husband." May 2009. Web.

December 7 2010
<http://www.answerology.com/index.aspx/question/26 60448_ladies-do-you-always-correct-you-husband.html>

7. Smith, Hyrum, W. The 10 Natural Laws of Successful Time and Life Management - Proven Strategies for Increased Productivity and Inner Peace." New York: Warner Books, Inc., 1994. pp. 179.

8. Elgin, Suzette, H., Ph.D. The Gentle Art of Verbal Self-Defense at Work. Paramus, New Jersey: Prentice Hall, Inc., 2000. pp. 316-317.

9. Patterson, Kerry et al. Crucial Conversations: tools for talking when stakes are high. New York: McGraw-Hill, 2002. pp. 48.

10. Cava, Roberta. Dealing with Difficult People - How to Deal with Nasty Customers, Demanding Bosses and Annoying Co-workers. New York: Firefly Books, 2004. pp. 88.

11. Evans, Gary, "So, What Do I Want?." Web. December 12 2010
<http://www.buzzle.com/articles/so-what-do-i-want.html>

12. Lefcourt, Herbert, M. Humor - The Psychology of Living Bouyantly. New York: Kluwer Academic / Plenum Publishers, 2001. pp. 134.

13. Jung, Carl, G. The Undiscovered Self. Boston: Atlantic Monthly Press - Little, Brown and Company, 1957. pp. 104.

14. Marshall, Evan. The Eyes Have It - Revealing Their Power, Messages, and Secrets. New York: Kensington Publishing Corp., 2003. pp. 27.

15. Lilley, Roy. Dealing with Difficult People. London: Kogan Page, 2004. pp. 5.

16. Brinkman, Rick and Kirschner, Rick. Dealing with people you can't stand: how to bring out the best in

people at their worst. New York: McGraw Hill, 2002. pp. 97-100.

17. Blog/Forum Posting, "Key to Dealing with Difficult People". Web. December 2 2010
<http://www.hofungyee.byethost4.com/agg-task.htm>

18. Nichols, Michael, D., PH.D. The Lost Art of Listening. New York: The Guilford Press, 1995. pp. 10.

19. Bolton, Robert, Ph.D. People Skills: how to assert yourself, listen to others, and resolve conflicts. New York: Simon & Schuster, Inc., 1979. pp. 15.

20. Blog/Forum Posting, "How To Deal With People Who Dominate Conversation." September 2010. Web. December 12 2010
<http://www.howcast.com/videos/394185-How-To-Deal-With-People-Who-Dominate-Conversation/>

21. Pryor, Tom. "Criticism ... gain that's Worth the Pain." Web. January 13 2011
<http://www.icms.net/criticism.htm>

22. Nations, Kenneth, H. III. "Dealing with know-it-alls - even if you are one yourself." Web. January 13 2011 < http://findarticles.com/p/articles/mi_m3230/is_n10_v22/ai_ 9011272/pg_2/>

23. Hayden, Scott. "How to Deal With Know-It-All Personalities." December 2009. Web. December 2 2010 <http://www.suite101.com/content/how-to-deal-with-knowitall personalities-a182170>

24. Benjamin, Susan. Perfect Phrases for Dealing with Difficult People. New York: McGraw-Hill Professional, 2007. pp. 4.

25. Derbyshire, David. "Solved: Mystery of how sharks can smell a drop of blood from quarter of a mile away." June 2010. Web. January 13 2011
<http://www.dailymail.co.uk/sciencetech/article-

1285652/Mystery-sharks-astonishing-sense-smell-solved.html>

26. Hadfield, Sue and Hasson, Gill. How to be Assertive in Any Situation. New Jersey: Prentice Hall Life, 2010. pp. 7.

27. Bolton, Robert, Ph.D. People Skills: how to assert yourself, listen to others, and resolve conflicts. New York: Simon & Schuster, Inc., 1979. pp. 12.

28. Corey, Gerald, and Corey, Marianne, S. I Never Knew I Had a Choice. Pacific Grove, California: Brooks/Cole Publishing Company, 2007. pp. 279.

29. Beier, Ernst, G. Dr. and Valens, Evans, G. People Reading - How We Control Others, How They Control Us. Lanham, Maryland: Scarborough House, 1992. pp. 28.

30. Gallo, Carmine. "Body Language: A Key to Success in the Workplace." February 2007. Web. January 13 2011 <http://finance.yahoo.com/career-work/article/102425/Body_Language:_A_Key_to_Success_in_the_Workplace>

31. Glass, Lillian, Ph.D. Complete Idiots Guide To - Verbal Self-Defense. Indianapolis, Indiana:
   Alpha Books, 1999. pp. 139-141.

32. Jung, Carl, G. The Undiscovered Self. Boston: Atlantic Monthly Press - Little, Brown and Company, 1957. pp. 89.

33. The Economist, "Chattering classes - The rules for verbal exchanges are surprisingly enduring." December 2006. Web. December 16 2010 <http://www.economist.com/node/
    8345491?story_id=8345491>

34. Watson, Robert. "Email Abuse - How to Stop Online Harassment." July 2007. Web. December 15 2010 <http://www.associatedcontent.com/article/291034/email_abuse_how_to_stop_online_harassment.html?cat=35>

35. Internetlawtoday.com. "Email & SPAM." Web. December 15 2010
   <http://www.internetlawtoday.com/email.html>

About the Author

Joe Ike is the pseudonym for Joseph Ike Afeli. He lives in Dallas. His other book, a work of fiction, is titled Human Traffickers. His other interests include running and cooking.

Made in the USA
Middletown, DE
24 November 2014